THE
TEQUILA
1000

The Ultimate Collection of Tequila Cocktails, Recipes, Facts and Resources

Ray Foley

SOURCEBOOKS, INC.
NAPERVILLE, ILLINOIS

Published by Sourcebooks, Inc.
P.O. Box 4410, Naperville, Illinois 60567-4410
(630) 961-3900
Fax: (630) 961-2168
www.sourcebooks.com

Library of Congress Cataloging-in-Publication Data

Foley, Ray.
  The tequila 1000 : the ultimate collection of tequila cocktails, recipes, facts, and resources / Ray Foley.
      p. cm.
  Includes index.
  ISBN 978-1-4022-1180-5 (trade pbk.)
  1. Cocktails. 2. Tequila. I. Title. II. Title: Tequila one thousand. III. Title: Tequila thousand.
TX951.F59458 2008
641.2'5--dc22

                                        2007042004

Printed and bound in the United States of America.
BG 10 9 8 7 6 5 4 3 2 1

DEDICATION

This book is dedicated to Jaclyn, Marie, and Ryan Foley, and to
the other tribe, Raymond, William, and Amy
And to
All the great readers of *Bartender Magazine* and
www.bartender.com

CONTENTS

ACKNOWLEDGMENTS

We would like to thank the following for their assistance in the completion of this book:

Vic Morrison at McCormick Distilling

Greg Cohen at the Richard Group in Dallas

Michelle Roux at Crillon Importers

Jim Nikolaat at Crillon Importers

Eileen at WebWiser Inc. (www.WebWiser.com)

The great folks at:

Diego

Jose Cuervo

Sauza Tequila Import Company

Tabasco

The Food Group

Skyy Spirits

Tarantula tequila

Barton Brands

Agavero

Cointreau

Matusalem rum

Coco Lopez

Bacardi

Brown-Forman

Pernod Ricard

. . . and all the other tequila companies that assisted in the completion of *Tequila 1000*.

To:

Erin Mackey, for her assistance, being the best, and continuing her education

Loretta Natiello, for being my best friend

Jimmy Zazzali, for being a great bartender and friend

Sara Kase, for her outstanding editing

Matt Wojciak, John Cowan, Mike Cammarano, Marvin Solomon, and of course the great Peter Lynch, for all of their assistance

Also, to all those who submitted recipes to www.bartender.com and the readers of *Bartender Magazine*.

And to all the great bartenders in America who have served me— you are the best!

INTRODUCTION

Welcome to the world of tequila. *The Tequila 1000* gives you all the information you need to know about tequila, from its history to cocktail recipes, food recipes, and over 100 websites about tequila.

Tequila is one of the most called-for cocktail ingredients. There are over 100 different tequilas on the market. We'll provide you with many ideas on how to use your personal favorite.

Whether you are a home bartender or a professional bartender, you will find *The Tequila 1000* a great reference for your exploration of tequila. Have fun, but remember this is tequila.

Some recipes will have the same ingredients but different names. Sorry, but I tried to give every product and bartender a fair shake.

A few notes on the recipes:

Sugar-free juice or diet pop can be substituted in any drink. For example, if a recipe calls for lemonade, feel free to use sugar-free lemonade; if a recipe calls for tonic, feel free to use diet tonic.

For martinis containing vermouth, the less vermouth, the drier the martini.

Enjoy, and please drink in moderation!

For more information on bartending, visit www.bartender.com

50
FACTS ABOUT TEQUILA

All tequila is from Mexico.

It must be produced in two regions of Mexico:
    All regions surrounding Tequila,
    Or the region of Tepatitlan.

Tequila is made from the agave plant.

Pulque (agave), was thought to be a gift from the gods.

An agave farmer is called a campesino.

Agave is also known as maguey (muh-gay).

It is harvested by a person with special skills, called the jimador.

The jimador uses a sharp, paddle-shaped blade known as a coa.

He slashes off the leaves and reveals the pina.

The pinas are cooked with water.

The resulting mixture, aquamel, is used for fermenting.

Traditionally, a pot is used for the distillation of tequila.

Juices ferment for thirty to forty-eight hours.

Juices are distilled twice.

Tequila must be at least 51 percent agave.

Some tequilas are 100 percent agave (blue).

Agave are harvested when they are eight to twelve years old.

Tequila was first distilled near the city of Tequila.

The city of Tequila is in the Mexican state of Jalisco.

Tequila was first mass-produced in Guadalajara, Mexico.

Most tequilas are 70 to 110 proof.

Don Pedro Sanchez de Tagle was the first person to mass-produce tequila.

The first person granted a distiller license was Jose Cuervo in 1795.

In 1805, a distillery was established that would become Sauza.

There are five types of tequila:
    Ora (gold), unaged tequila.
    Blanco (white), not aged, freshly distilled.
    Reposado (rested), aged a minimum of two months but less than a year in oak barrels.
    Anejo (vintage), aged minimum one year but less than three years in oak barrels.
    Extra anejo (extra aged), aged a minimum one to three years in oak barrels.

Extra Anejo is a brand-new type of tequila established in March 2006.

Aging changes the color of tequila.

The longer the aging, the darker the color.

Extra Anejo tends to be darker.

Sometimes caramel is used for color.

There are over one hundred distilleries in Mexico.

Over 2,100 brand names have been registered.

Tequileno is the name of a person trained in tequila production and history.

The worm is not in tequila.

The worm is in Mezcal.

"Con gusano" means "with worm."

The reason for the worm in mezcal is to prove high proof.

The term tequila was first printed in English in 1849.

Tequila became popular in the United States during the sixties.

The most popular tequila cocktail is the margarita.

The tequila shot is the second most popular way of drinking tequila.

The tequila shot is lemon, salt, and a shot of tequila.

Lick the salt, drink the tequila, bite the lemon.

3RD STREET PROMENADE

1⅓ oz. tequila
1½ oz. gin
⅓ oz. triple sec
½ oz. cinnamon schnapps
5 oz. orange juice

Put ingredients in a blender with ice. Blend well and pour into a tall chilled glass.

43 AMIGOS

2 oz. Don Alvaro tequila
½ oz. Licor 43
½ oz. triple sec
½ oz. lime juice
lime wedge for garnish

Shake and strain into a chilled martini glass. Garnish with lime wedge.

ABSOLUT TEQUILA

1 oz. tequila
1 oz. Absolut vodka
4 oz. orange juice
lemon slice for garnish

Shake well and serve with plenty of crushed ice. Garnish with lemon slice.

ACAPULCO

2 oz. tequila
2 oz. pineapple juice
Sprite or 7UP

Pour first two ingredients into a glass and fill with Sprite or 7UP. Serve in an old-fashioned glass with ice.

ACAPULCO CLAM DIGGER

2 oz. tequila
3 oz. tomato juice*
3 oz. clam juice*
½ tsp. horseradish
several dashes Tabasco
several dashes Worcestershire sauce
dash lemon juice

Mix thoroughly with cracked ice in a double old fashioned glass. Top with lemon juice.
    *Clamato juice may be used in place of clam and tomato juice.

ACAPULCO LICORICE MARGARITA

1 oz. tequila
1 oz. Cointreau
½ oz. lime juice
1 oz. Galliano
1 tsp. Tabasco green pepper sauce
1 tsp. salt

Dip rim of glass into Tabasco sauce and rim with salt. Shake remaining ingredients with ice and strain into a salt-rimmed glass.

ACID TRIP

½ oz. tequila
1½ oz. Midori
½ oz. gin
½ oz. vodka
½ oz. rum

Shake with ice and strain into a cocktail glass.

ADAM BOMB

1 part tequila
1 part rum
1 part vodka
½ part Cointreau
¼ slice lemon or lime
½ glass ice
salt or sugar to rim glass
1–2 parts fruit juice
lemon or lime slice for garnish

Blend with ice until smooth. Rim glass with sugar or salt, pour into the glass, and garnish with a lemon or lime slice.

AGAVERO SUNSET

2 oz. Agavero tequila
1 large scoop vanilla ice cream

Float tequila over the top of the ice cream. Enjoy with a 1-oz. side shot of Agavero if desired.

ALABAMA SLAMMER

1 oz. tequila
1 oz. Kahlua
2 oz. Sprite

Shake first two ingredients with ice and strain into a lowball glass. Top with Sprite.

ALAMO SPLASH

1½ oz. tequila
1 oz. orange juice
½ oz. pineapple juice
splash lemon-lime soda

Stir and strain into a Collins glass with cracked ice.

ALICE IN WONDERLAND

½ oz. tequila
½ oz. Grand Marnier
½ oz. Tia Maria

Serve as a shooter, in an old-fashioned glass.

ALMENDRADO SODA

2 oz. Reserva del Señor Almendrado tequila
soda to fill

Pour Reserva del Señor Almendrado into a glass and fill with soda.

AMARETTO STONE SOUR # 3

1 oz. tequila
1 oz. amaretto
2 oz. sour mix
splash orange juice
orange slice for garnish
cherry for garnish

Shake first three ingredients with ice and strain into a highball glass. Add orange juice. Garnish with an orange slice and a cherry.

AMBASSADOR

2 oz. tequila
4 oz. orange juice
1 oz. sugar syrup

Pour the tequila into a glass, add ice and orange juice. Add sugar syrup to sweeten.

AMBER'S REVENGE

1 oz. tequila
1 oz. scotch
1 oz. rum
root beer (preferably A&W)

Mix over ice in a highball glass and fill with root beer.

AMIGAZO

1½ oz. Buen Amigo tequila
2 oz. pineapple juice
dash Rose's lime juice
few drops grenadine

Shake over crushed ice, then add grenadine.

AMOR

2 oz. tequila
½ oz. orange curaçao or Cointreau

Serve in an old fashioned glass with ice.

AMOR-A

2 oz. tequila
½ oz. orange curaçao
½ oz. amaretto

Serve in an old fashioned glass with ice.

ANEJO ALEXANDER

1½ oz. Patron anejo tequila
1 oz. XO Café
1 oz. half-and-half or milk
¼ tsp. grated nutmeg

Shake the first three ingredients with ice and strain into a cocktail glass. Garnish with grated nutmeg.

ANEJO TEQUILA NEAT

2 oz. Don Julio Añejo tequila

Serve in a rocks glass.

ANGEL'S BESO

1½ oz. Gran Centenario anejo tequila
Ghiradelli hot chocolate

Pour tequila into a glass and top with Ghiradelli hot chocolate.

ANGEL'S MARGARITA

2 oz. Gran Centenario Plata tequila
¾ oz. Grand Marnier
2 oz. fresh-squeezed lime juice
1 tsp. simple syrup
lime wedge for garnish

Shake vigorously over ice in a mixing glass. Strain into a prechilled martini glass or pour over ice in a cocktail highball glass. Garnish with a lime wedge.

ANGEL'S PASSION

1½ oz. Gran Centenario Plata tequila
1 oz. sweetened passion fruit puree
1 oz. fresh orange juice
1 tsp. simple syrup
flamed orange twist for garnish

Shake vigorously in a mixing glass. Garnish with a flamed orange twist.

ANGEL'S TEMPTATION

1¾ oz. Gran Centenario Plata tequila
3½ oz. fresh apple juice
½ oz. fresh-squeezed orange juice
¼ oz. squeezed lime wedge
green apple slice for garnish

Shake vigorously over ice in a mixing glass. Strain over fresh ice into a Collins or highball glass. Garnish with a green apple slice.

ANGRY PARROT

1 part Corazon blanco tequila
1 part apple schnapps
splash fresh lime juice
lemon twist for garnish

Garnish with a lemon twist.

APOLLO

1½ oz. tequila
1 oz. Galliano
1 oz. blue curaçao
cream to top

Shake the first three ingredients with ice and strain into a cocktail glass. Float the cream on top.

AQUA TINI

1½ oz. Tarantula Azul tequila
¾ oz. Cointreau
lime squeeze
lemon squeeze
½ oz. simple syrup
lemon slice for garnish
lime slice for garnish

Salt rim of glass. Shake vigorously with ice in a mixing glass and strain into a martini glass. Garnish with a lemon and lime slice and serve.

ARIZONA AZTEC

1 oz. Cuervo gold tequila
1 oz. Bacardi Limon
½ oz. Captain Morgan's spiced rum
7 oz. Coca-Cola

Stir well in a highball glass.

ASSASSIN

½ oz. tequila
½ oz. Jack Daniel's whisky
½ oz. peppermint schnapps
Coca-Cola

Pour first three ingredients into a glass and fill with Coca-Cola. Mix and serve in a cocktail glass.

AVOCADO MARGARITA

1½ oz. silver tequila
½ oz. Cointreau
1 oz. lime juice
½ oz. lemon juice
¼ cup diced ripe avocado
1 oz. half-and-half
1 tsp. sugar
½ cup ice
lime slice for garnish
avocado slice for garnish

Combine in a blender with ice and blend until smooth. Pour into a chilled cocktail glass. Garnish with a lime slice and avocado slice.

AZTEC GOLD MARTINI

1 oz. Jose Cuervo gold tequila
1 oz. Absolut
½ oz. Mount Gay rum
1 oz. pineapple juice

Stir with ice in a mixing glass and strain into a martini glass.

AZTEC SKY

1¾ oz. Buen Amigo tequila
¾ oz. blue curaçao

Serve in a shot glass.

BAD ATTITUDE

½ oz. tequila
½ oz. rum
½ oz. vodka
½ oz. gin
½ oz. triple sec
1 oz. amaretto
½ oz. grenadine
Equal parts:
pineapple juice
orange juice
cranberry juice

Shake and pour into a tall glass.

BAHA FOG

1½ oz. tequila
1 beer (Corona)
¼ lime

Open a Corona and fill it to the top with tequila. Squeeze ¼ lime on top.

BAILEYS TEQUILA CREAM

½ oz. Jose Cuervo Tradicional tequila
2 oz. Baileys Irish cream

Serve over ice or in a shot glass.

BARKING SPIDER

1½ oz. tequila (preferably Tarantula Azul tequila)
½ oz. blue curaçao
¾ oz. Bacardi 151 Proof rum
dash triple sec
dash sour mix
splash orange juice

Serve over ice in a Collins glass, or blend for a frozen version.

BAY CITY BOMBER

½ oz. tequila
½ oz. vodka
½ oz. rum
½ oz. gin
½ oz. triple sec
1 oz. orange juice
1 oz. pineapple juice
1 oz. cranberry juice
1 oz. sour mix
¼ oz. Bacardi 151 Proof rum
cherry for garnish
orange slice for garnish

Blend all except 151 rum with one cup of ice until smooth and pour into a parfait glass. Float 151 rum and garnish with a cherry and an orange slice.

BB GUN

1 oz. tequila
1 oz. vodka
½ oz. sambuca
splash lime juice
splash lime cordial
splash club soda

Serve in a frosted Collins glass.

BEACH

1¼ oz. Buen Amigo tequila
¾ oz. Cointreau
3 oz. cranberry juice
lemon wedge for garnish

Stir. Garnish with a lemon wedge.

BEAUTY AND THE BEAST

1 oz. Tequila Rose
1 oz. Jagermeister

Mix and strain into a shot glass.

BEE STING

1½ oz. Patron reposado tequila
½ oz. Marie Brizard crème de cassis
½ oz. clover honey syrup
juice of 1 lime, hand extracted
2 oz. fresh-squeezed blood orange juice
blackberries for garnish
raspberries for garnish

Shake with ice until well blended. Strain into a 14-oz. goblet over ice.
Garnish with blackberries and raspberries.

BEERGARITA

1½ oz. tequila
½ oz. triple sec
1 oz. lemon juice
6 oz. cold draft beer
splash lime juice
salt to rim mug

Rub rim of beer mug with lemon juice, dip rim in salt. Shake all
ingredients with ice, strain into the salt-rimmed mug. Fill with cold draft
beer and serve.

BENELYN

1 oz. tequila
1 oz. Southern Comfort
½ oz. peach schnapps
½ bottle Hoopers Hooch (or similar lemon alcopop)
½ can Red Bull Energy Drink
cranberry juice

Pour in the first three ingredients, then add the lemon alcopop and Red Bull. Top with cranberry juice to about 1 cm below the top of the glass.

BERRY MEDLEY

1½ oz. Patron silver
¾ oz. Chambord
1 oz. fresh sweet and sour
1 oz. pineapple juice
3 fresh raspberries (plus 1 for garnish)
peach schnapps to float
pineapple spear for garnish

Shake all ingredients with ice. Strain and serve over ice. Garnish with pineapple spear with a fresh raspberry on top.

BERTA'S SPECIAL

2 oz. tequila
1 tsp. honey
6 dashes orange bitters
juice of 1 lime
sparkling water to fill
lime slice for garnish

Shake first four ingredients vigorously with ice and strain into a Collins glass with ice cubes. Fill with sparkling water and garnish with a slice of lime.

BERTHA

1¼ oz. tequila
½ tsp. red wine
1¼ tsp. sugar
1 tbsp. fresh lemon or lime juice
lemon peel
cherry for garnish

Serve in a chilled highball glass with ice. Twist lemon peel over drink and drop in. Garnish with cherry.

BESITOS

1½ parts tequila Tezón anejo
1 part Limoncello
1 part Stoli Citron
dash grenadine
juice of ½ lemon
gummy heart for garnish

Shake well and serve in a martini glass. Garnish with a gummy heart.

BIG JOHN'S STRAWBERRY MANGO MARGARITA

4 oz. tequila (premium)
5 oz. triple sec (preferably Du Bouchett)
12½ oz. mango juice (preferably Jumex or Kern's canned mango juice)
1½ cups strawberries (fresh or frozen but NOT in sugar or juice)

Place ice, strawberries, tequila, triple sec, and mango juice in a blender (in order). Blend on "ice crush" and then on "frappe." Serve in a margarita glass. Serves 2 or 3.

BIG RED HOOTER

1 oz. tequila
¾ oz. amaretto
pineapple juice
1 oz. grenadine
cherry for garnish

Build first two ingredients over ice in a Collins glass and fill with pineapple juice. Add grenadine and garnish with a cherry.

BIG SPENDER

1½ oz. Gran Centenario anejo tequila
1 oz. liqueur creole
¾ oz. blood orange juice
Cristal Rose champagne
orange peel for garnish
flamed orange zest for garnish

Pour first three ingredients into a bar glass with ice and stir to chill. Strain into a chilled champagne flute and top with the Rose champagne. Garnish with spiral of orange peel and a flamed orange zest.

BILLIONAIRE'S MARGARITA

1½ oz. Jose Cuervo Reserva de la Familia tequila
½ oz. Grand Marnier Cuvée du Centenaire
2 oz. freshly squeezed lime juice
5 oz. crushed ice

Shake well with ice and strain into a glass with ice. Garnish with a lime wedge.

BITTERSWEET STEVE ON THE ROCKS

1 oz. Sauza tequila
1 oz. Jack Daniel's whisky
½ oz. Jagermeister
cran-grape juice (preferably Langers 100 Percent cranberry grape juice)

Pour first three ingredients into a highball glass filled halfway with ice and fill with cran-grape juice. Stir.

BLACK CAT

1 part Jose Cuervo tequila
1 part amaretto

Serve as a shot.

BLACK MEXICAN (HOT)

1½ oz. tequila
1½ oz. Kahlua
⅛ oz. Tabasco

Serve as a shot.

BLACKBERRY TEQUILA

2 oz. tequila
½ oz. crème de cassis
1 oz. lemon juice

Shake with ice and pour into a chilled glass.

BLANCO MARTINI

2 parts Chinaco blanco tequila
1 part dry vermouth
1 part sweet vermouth
maraschino cherry for garnish

Stir with ice and strain into a salt-rimmed, chilled martini glass. Garnish with a maraschino cherry.

BLEEDING WEASEL

½ oz. tequila
½ oz. vodka
½ oz. rum
½ oz. gin
½ oz. triple sec
½ oz. brandy
½ oz. Malibu rum
2 oz. beer (preferably pilsner)
8 oz. orange juice
½ oz. Rose's lime juice
⅛ oz. grenadine

Mix well and serve over ice. Makes 2 12-oz. cocktails.

BLITZ

1 part tequila
1 part orange juice
1 part triple sec
1 part Southern Comfort peach liqueur
1 part grenadine syrup
1 part lemon juice

Shake with ice. Strain or serve with ice.

BLOODY BULL

2 oz. tequila
½ glass tomato juice
½ glass beef bouillon
celery stalk for garnish
lime wheel for garnish

Pour into a highball glass over ice. Stir and add a squeeze of lemon. Garnish with a celery stalk and a lime wheel.

BLOODY HURRICANE

2 oz. tequila
1 can 7UP
½ oz. grenadine

Pour tequila over ice into a highball glass. Add 7UP to the top and add grenadine. Allow to chill for a few seconds.

BLOODY MARIA

2 oz. tequila
3 oz. tomato juice or V8 juice
dash lemon juice
dash Tabasco
dash celery salt
dash salt
dash pepper
lime slice or celery stick for garnish

Shake with cracked ice and strain into a Collins glass over ice cubes. Garnish with a slice of lime or celery stick.

BLOODY MATADOR

2 oz. Cuervo gold tequila
2 oz. Red Bull Energy Drink
1 oz. triple sec
3 oz. limeade (frozen)
1 oz. grenadine

Blend with ice until slushy and serve in a cocktail glass.

BLOODY PEPE

2 oz. Pepe Lopez tequila
2 oz. tomato juice
dash lemon juice
dash hot sauce
lemon slice or celery stick for garnish

Pour into a tall glass over ice cubes. Garnish with a slice of lemon or a celery stick.

BLUE AGAVE MIST

1½–2 oz. premium silver or anejo tequila
twist of lime
crushed ice

Rim the edge of an old-fashioned glass with the lime twist and fill with crushed ice. Add the tequila and the twist of lime.

BLUE SEVEN

2 oz. Tarantula Azul tequila
4 oz. lemon-lime soda
⅛ oz. blue curaçao
lime wedge for garnish

Build first two ingredients in a 14-oz. Collins glass over ice. Top with blue curaçao. Garnish with a lime wedge.

BLUE SEX

1 oz. tequila
1 oz. blue curaçao
½ oz. Midori
½ oz. Cointreau

Shake with ice and strain into a cocktail glass.

BLUE SHARK

1 oz. white tequila
1 oz. Sobieski vodka
4 dashes blue curaçao

Shake with ice and strain into a chilled old-fashioned glass.

BLUE SMOKE

1¼ oz. Jose Cuervo tequila
½ oz. blue curaçao
3 oz. orange juice

Pour tequila and orange juice into a chilled wine glass with finely crushed ice. Stir. Float blue curaçao on top.

BOMSHEL

1 oz. Tequila Rose
1 oz. McCormick vodka

Serve as a shot.

BON VOYAGE

1 oz. Jose Cuervo tequila
1 oz. gin
dash lemon juice
dash blue curaçao

Pour the first two ingredients over ice into a cocktail glass. Then mix in a dash of lemon juice and dash of blue curaçao. Stir lightly. Best when drunk with a straw.

BONBON

1½ oz. tequila
1½ oz. Cointreau
dash grenadine

Pour into a rocks glass.

BOOTLEGGER

1½ oz. tequila
1 oz. Jack Daniel's whisky
½ oz. Southern Comfort

Stir in a lowball glass.

BORDER CROSSING

1½ oz. tequila
2 tsp. lime juice
1 tsp. lemon juice
4 oz. cola
lime wedge for garnish

Build in a highball glass and stir well. Add cola. Garnish with a lime wedge.

BOWL HUGGER

1 oz. tequila (white)
1 oz. gin
1 oz. rum
1 oz. Cointreau
dash Rose's lime juice
Equal parts:
orange juice
pineapple juice
sweet and sour mix

Build over ice in a large cup and stir.

BRAVE BULL

2 oz. tequila
½ oz. coffee liqueur

Pour tequila and coffee liqueur over ice cubes in a rocks glass. Stir.

BROKEN NOSE

1 oz. tequila (golden)
2 oz. grenadine
1½ oz. advocaat
lemonade to fill

Pour first two ingredients into a highball glass and mix. Add advocaat, making sure it does not properly mix and remains phlegm-like. Fill with lemonade.

BROTHEL

1¼ oz. Tequila Rose
¾ oz. crème de menthe (mint liqueur)
milk to fill

Build in a highball glass packed with ice. Fill up with ice cold milk.

BRUJA MEXICANA

½ oz. Agavero tequila liqueur
½ oz. Strega liqueur
soda water to fill
dash sugar syrup
lemon to rim glass
sugar to rim glass

Blend the first two ingredients with crushed ice. Moisten the rim of a Collins glass with lemon and frost with sugar. Add a little sugar syrup and fill with soda.

BUMBLEBEE KEELA

2 oz. tequila
1½ oz. sour mix
1 tbsp. honey

Shake well with ice. Strain and add ice.

BUNNY BONANZA

2 oz. tequila
1 oz. apple brandy
3 dashes triple sec
½ oz. fresh lemon juice
¾ tsp. maple syrup
lemon slice for garnish

Shake with ice and strain into a chilled old-fashioned glass. Garnish with a lemon slice.

BUTTAFUOCO

2 oz. white tequila
½ oz. Galliano
½ oz. cherry juice
½ oz. fresh lemon juice
club soda to fill
maraschino cherry for garnish

Shake first four ingredients with ice and strain over ice cubes into a highball glass. Fill with club soda, stir gently, and garnish with a maraschino cherry.

CABO

1½ oz. Jose Cuervo tequila
3 oz. pineapple juice
¼ oz. lime juice

Shake well in a shaker half-filled with ice cubes. Strain into a cocktail glass.

CACTUS BANGER

1¼ oz. tequila
2½ oz. orange juice
½ oz. Galliano

Build first two ingredients in a Collins glass with ice. Float Galliano.

CACTUS BERRY

1¼ oz. tequila
1¼ oz. red wine
1 oz. triple sec
6½ oz. sour mix
splash lemon-lime soda
dash lime juice
salt to rim glass

Salt the rim of a large margarita cocktail glass. Shake with ice and pour into the salted glass.

CACTUS BITE

2 oz. tequila
2 tsp. triple sec
2 tsp. Drambuie
2 oz. lemon juice
1½ tsp. fine sugar
dash bitters

In a shaker half-filled with ice cubes, combine all of the ingredients. Shake well. Strain into a cocktail glass.

CACTUS KICKER

2 oz. tequila
2 oz. sour mix
3 drops Tabasco
lime squeeze to taste
lime wheel for garnish

Pour into a 12-oz. highball glass packed with ice. Stir and serve in a salt-rimmed glass. Garnish with a lime wheel.

CAFE DEL PRADO

1½ oz. tequila
2 tsp. instant cocoa
1 tsp. instant coffee
whipped cream
powdered cinnamon or nutmeg

Put coffee and cocoa in a mug and fill with boiling water. Add tequila, mix well, and top with whipped cream. Grate a little cinnamon or nutmeg on top.

CAIPICUERVO

1½ oz. Jose Cuervo Especial tequila
2 tsp. sugar
¼ oz. lime juice
2 lime wedges

Place sugar in a glass and add lime wedges. Break down lime with muddler or back of a spoon so juice is absorbed by sugar. Then pour in the tequila and lime juice.

CALIFORNIA DREAM

2 oz. tequila
1 oz. sweet vermouth
½ oz. dry vermouth
cherry for garnish

Pour into a mixing glass half-filled with ice cubes and stir well. Strain into a cocktail glass and garnish with a cherry.

CAM2 RACING FUEL

1 oz. tequila
1 oz. whisky
½ oz. Bacardi rum
½ oz. Everclear
Coca-Cola

Mix over ice in a Collins glass and top with Coca-Cola.

CAMEL PISS

1 oz. tequila
1 oz. Bacardi Dark rum
1 oz. Ouzo
3 oz. beer (preferably Canadian beer)
Mountain Dew

Pour the first four ingredients into a large glass and top with Mountain Dew.

CAMINO REAL

1½ oz. Buen Amigo tequila
½ oz. banana liqueur
1 oz. orange juice
dash lime juice
dash coconut milk
lime slice for garnish

Shake or blend. Garnish with a lime slice.

CAMPER

1½ oz. tequila
2 oz. orange juice
2 oz. pineapple juice
½ oz. Chambord

Pour the first three ingredients into a highball glass almost filled with ice cubes. Stir well. Drop the Chambord into the center of the drink.

CAN CAN

1½ oz. white tequila
½ oz. dry vermouth
4 oz. grapefruit juice
½ tsp. sugar syrup
orange slice for garnish

Mix all ingredients in a shaker or blender with cracked ice. Pour into a double old-fashioned glass. Garnish with orange slice.

CANE TOAD

1 oz. tequila
1 oz. vodka
½ oz. cherry brandy
3 oz. soda water

Pour first three ingredients into a 10-oz. glass and fill with soda water.

CANTARITA

1½ oz. blanco tequila
½ oz. orange juice
½ oz. lemon juice
½ oz. grapefruit juice
⅛ oz. lime juice
½ oz. grapefruit soda
orange, lemon, grapefruit, and lime slices for garnish

Pour into a glass with ice and garnish with an orange, lemon, grape-fruit, and lime slice.

CARABINIERI

1 oz. tequila
¾ oz. Galliano
½ oz. Cointreau
1 tsp. Rose's lime juice
3 oz. orange juice
1 egg yolk
red cherry for garnish
green cherry for garnish
lime slice for garnish

Shake and strain into a Collins glass over ice. Garnish with a red and a green cherry and a lime slice.

CARAMBA!

2 oz. white tequila
3 oz. grapefruit juice
club soda to top

Mix first two ingredients in a shaker or blender with cracked ice. Pour into a tall highball glass. Top with club soda.

CAROLINA

2 oz. tequila gold
1 oz. half-and-half
1 tsp. vanilla extract
1 tsp. grenadine
1 egg white
cinnamon for sprinkling
cherry for garnish

Shake vigorously with ice and strain into a cocktail glass. Sprinkle with cinnamon and garnish with a cherry.

CATALINA MARGARITA

1½ oz. Jose Cuervo tequila
1 oz. peach schnapps
1 oz. blue curaçao
4 oz. sour mix
salt to rim glass

Shake well with ice and strain into salt-rimmed glass.

CATALINA MARGARITA #2

1½ oz. XXX tequila
peach schnapps
1 oz. blue curaçao
4 oz. sour mix

Shake with cracked ice and strain into a chilled cocktail or margarita glass.

CAVALIER

1½ oz. Buen Amigo tequila
½ oz. Galliano
1½ oz. orange juice
½ oz. cream

Blend with crushed ice and strain into cocktail glass.

CAZADORES CANTARITA

1½ parts Cazadores reposado tequila
½ parts peach juice
½ parts orange juice
½ parts grapefruit juice
2 parts grapefruit soda
pineapple wedge for garnish
cherry for garnish

Shake with ice and strain into tall glass. If desired, add splash of grenadine and a sugar rim. Garnish with a pineapple wedge or a cherry.

CAZADORES MEXICAN MARTINI COCKTAIL

2 parts Cazadores reposado tequila
½ parts sweet and sour
1 splash of jalapeño juice
1 splash of fresh lime juice
jalapeño or jalapeño-stuffed olives for garnish

Shake with ice and strain into a chilled martini glass. Garnish with jalapeño or jalapeño-stuffed olives.

C. C. KAZI

1 oz. tequila
1 oz. cranberry juice
1 tsp. lime juice
splash cola

Shake first three ingredients with ice and strain into a cordial glass. Top with cola.

C. C. KAZI SHOOTER

1 oz. tequila
2 oz. cranberry juice
1 tsp. lime juice

Shake well with ice and strain into cocktail glass.

CELEBRITA

1½ oz. tequila (recommended: Herradura silver)
2 oz. celery juice (about 2 stalks celery, juiced and strained)
1 oz. fresh-squeezed lemon juice
1 oz. simple syrup
celery salt to rim glass
cherry tomato for garnish
celery stalk for garnish

Shake first three ingredients vigorously with ice and pour into a chilled martini glass rimmed with celery salt. Garnish with a cherry tomato and a stalk of celery and serve immediately.

CHAMPION MARGARITA

2 oz. Jose Cuervo tequila
2 oz. can limeade
2 oz. beer of your choice

Blend first two ingredients with ice. Top with beer.

CHAPALA

1½ oz. Olmeca tequila
1 tbsp. orange juice
1 tbsp. lemon juice
dash triple sec
2 tbsp. grenadine
orange slice for garnish

Shake with ice and strain into old fashioned-glass over ice cubes. Garnish with a slice of orange.

CHAPULTEPEC CASTLE

1½ oz. tequila
¼ oz. Grand Marnier
4 oz. orange juice
orange slice for garnish

Mix all ingredients in a shaker or blender with cracked ice and pour into a double old-fashioned glass. Garnish with an orange slice.

CHARLEY GOODLEG

1½ oz. tequila
1 oz. Galliano
3 oz. orange juice

Frost the rim of a glass with sugar. Shake the first two ingredients with ice, then top up with orange juice and stir.

THE CHECKER FLAG

2 oz. Tequila Rose
3 oz. milk

Combine over ice in a cocktail glass.

CHEKERS

1 oz. tequila
1 can beer

Pour the beer in a mug, drop in the shot of tequila, stir, and drink.

CHIHUAHUA

2 oz. tequila
grapefruit juice to fill
salt to rim glass

Pour tequila into a glass and fill with grapefruit juice. Salt rim of high-ball glass then add sip stick.

CHILE

1½ oz. tequila
½ oz. Bacardi rum
⅓ cup strawberry daiquiri mix
3 tbsp. lime juice
chili pepper

Blend first four ingredients with lots of ice. Take a bite out of the chili pepper and drink.

CHILI PEPPER MARGARITA

1¼ oz. Arandas tequila
¼ oz. Absolut Peppar vodka
¾ oz. Cointreau
¾ oz. lime juice
salt to rim glass
jalapeño for garnish

Pour ingredients into iced mixing glass. Shake and strain into salt-rimmed specialty glass. Top with jalapeño pepper.

CHINA GIRL

1½ oz. tequila (Jose 1800)
1½ oz. frost brandy (Christian Brothers)
1½ oz. Tequila Rose
6 oz. sweetened condensed milk

Blend with ice until smooth and pour into an exotic glass.

CHINACO AND TONIC

2 parts Chinaco reposado tequila
chilled tonic water to fill
coarse salt to rim glass
lime slice to rim glass
lime slice for garnish

Rub the rim of a highball glass with a lime slice and dip it into a bowl of coarse salt. Fill glass with ice and squeeze remaining lime juice into it. Add Chinaco reposado and stir. Fill with tonic water to taste. Garnish with a lime slice.

CHINACO SUNRISE

2 parts Chinaco anejo tequila
2 parts grenadine
orange juice to fill
pineapple wedge for garnish

Pour tequila into a chilled highball glass with ice. Fill with orange juice leaving room at the top. Stir. Slowly pour in the grenadine. Garnish with pineapple wedge.

CHOCKLIC

¾ oz. Buen Amigo tequila
¾ oz. Kahlua coffee liqueur
1 oz. orange juice

Shake and strain into a rocks glass.

CHOCOLATE CREAM SODA

1½ oz. Tequila Rose cocoa
½ oz. half-and-half
soda to fill
cherry for garnish

Build first two ingredients in a highball glass with ice and fill with soda. Garnish with speared cherry.

CHOCOLATE STRAWBERRY

1 oz. Tequila Rose
½ oz. milk
½ oz. chocolate liqueur

Fill with hot coffee and top with whipped cream.

CHONGO

2 oz. tequila
Orange soda

Pour tequila into a tall highball or Collins glass with ice and fill with orange soda. Stir gently. Garnish with a lime wedge.

CICADA

½ oz. Gran Patron platinum tequila
2¼ oz. Hangar One / St. George Spirits wasabi vodka
½ oz. Siberian Tiger European blood orange liqueur (chilled in freezer)
dash Angostura bitters
8 dashes Tabasco Green Jalapeño Pepper Sauce
2 drops balsamic vinegar
pinch finely ground fleur de sel

In a shaker, combine vodka, tequila, lime juice, bitters, Tabasco sauce, vinegar and salt over a few cubes of hard frozen ice. In a chilled cocktail glass, pour chilled blood orange liqueur to bottom of glass. Carefully layer on cocktail mixture. Garnish with a generous pinch of a confetti made of very finely minced baby chive, mint, and freshly grated ginger.

CINCO DE MAYO

2½ oz. tequila
1 oz. grenadine
1 oz. Rose's lime juice

Mix well with ice and strain into a chilled cocktail glass. Garnish with a lime wedge.

CINCO DE MAYO #2

1½ oz. El Mayor blanco tequila
¾ oz. Juarez triple sec
1¾ oz. cranberry juice

Shake well with ice and strain into a chilled martini glass. Garnish with a lime wedge.

CLAM DIGGER

2 oz. XXX tequila
3 oz. tomato juice
3 oz. clam juice
¾ tbsp. horseradish
Tabasco to taste
Worcestershire sauce to taste
splash lemon juice
lemon or lime slice for garnish

Mix all in a rocks glass with ice. Garnish with a lemon or lime slice.

THE CLASICO SHOT

2 oz. Jose Cuervo Clásico tequila
pinch salt
lime wedge

*Pour tequila into a shot glass. Lick skin between thumb and forefinger,
Sprinkle salt on moist skin. Drink shot all at once and quickly. Lick salt
and suck lime wedge.*

CLASSIC HOT MARGARITA

1½ oz. Herradura silver tequila
1 oz. Cointreau
juice of ½ lime
drop agave nectar
drop grenadine
drop blue curaçao
Tabasco to rim glass
salt to rim glass
lime slice for garnish
pineapple leaves for garnish

Shake first three ingredients over ice. Strain into a cocktail glass rimmed with Tabasco and salt. Garnish with a slice of lime and pineapple leaves.

CLEAR CELL

½ oz. tequila (light)
1 oz. lemon vodka
½ oz. Bacardi Limon
½ oz. dry gin
2 oz. lemon-lime soda
lime wedge for garnish

Shake first three ingredients with ice and strain into a highball glass. Top with soda and garnish with a lime wedge.

COCKTAIL ON THE ATTACK!

2 parts tequila
1 part Cointreau
1 part dry vermouth
1 lime
lime slice for garnish

Pour first three ingredients into a cocktail mixer. Squeeze in the juice from a lime, and add crushed ice. Shake vigorously. Serve in a champagne glass and garnish with a slice of lime.

COCO LOCO

2 oz. tequila
3 oz. pineapple juice
2 oz. coconut syrup
grated coconut
pineapple spear for garnish

Blend with crushed ice and pour into a tall glass. Garnish with a pineapple spear. If available, serve in a coconut shell.

COCONUT ALMOND MARGARITA

1¼ oz. Don Alvaro tequila
2½ oz. sweet and sour mix
½ oz. cream of coconut
¼ oz. amaretto liqueur
½ oz. fresh lime juice
lime slice for garnish

Shake. Garnish with a lime slice.

COCONUT CHOCOLATE TEQUILA

1½ oz. tequila
1 oz. Godiva liqueur
1 oz. cream
2 tsp. coconut cream
1 tsp. maraschino liqueur

Pour all ingredients into a blender with a half cup of ice. Blend for fifteen seconds. Pour into a medium sized cocktail glass and serve.

COCONUT COFFEE TEQUILA

1½ oz. tequila
1 oz. Kahlua
2 tsp. Coco Lopez
2 oz. cream
4 oz. crushed ice

Combine in a blender at a low speed for fifteen seconds. Strain and serve straight up.

COCONUT VANILLA TEQUILA

1½ oz. tequila
1 oz. Navan Vanilla liqueur
2 tsp. Coco Lopez
1 oz. cream
1 tsp. maraschino liqueur

Mix with crushed ice for 15 seconds in a blender. Strain into a cocktail glass.

COCOMISTICO

½ oz. Buen Amigo tequila
½ oz. Baileys Irish cream
½ oz. Godiva liqueur
1 oz. half-and-half

Shake and strain into a rocks glass.

COCOTEQ

1½ oz. tequila
½ oz. grenadine
1 oz. sour mix
sugar to rim glass

Shake with ice and strain into a cocktail glass. Frost the rim of the glass with sugar.

COLORADO SKIES

1 oz. tequila
1 oz. blue curaçao
5 oz. grapefruit juice

Pour into a highball glass.

COMMITMENT

1 oz. Jose Cuervo tequila
1 oz. bourbon
dash Tabasco

Shake. Serve on the rocks or as a shot.

COMPADRE

1½ oz. tequila
½ tsp. maraschino liqueur
1 tsp. grenadine
2 dashes orange bitters

Shake with ice and strain into a cocktail glass.

CONFETTI DROPS

1 oz. Jose Cuervo Especial tequila
½ oz. Goldschlager

Serve chilled in a shot glass.

COOL KID

1 part Jose Cuervo tequila
1 part vodka
1 part Sprite

Serve in a tall glass with ice.

CORAZÓN DE LEÓN

1½ parts Corazón de Agave reposado tequila
½ part triple sec or Cointreau
½ part fresh lime juice
½ part sour mix
splash orange juice
splash amaretto
salt to rim glass
lime slice for garnish

Shake first five ingredients and strain into a martini glass with a salted rim. Add a splash of amaretto as a floater. Garnish with a fresh lime slice.

CORAZÓN DE PECHE

1 part Corazón tequila
1 part peach liqueur
½ part Cointreau
splash fresh lime juice

Mix and serve on the rocks.

CORAZÓN ENCANTADO

1½ parts Corazón de Agave reposado tequila
¾ part peach brandy
splash raspberry liqueur
squeeze fresh lime juice
mint sprig for garnish

Mix in a shaker and strain into a martini glass. Garnish with a mint sprig.

CORAZÓN POM-TINI

1 part Corazón tequila
1 part pomegranate juice
1 part pom liqueur
splash sweet and sour mix

CORAZÓN PUNCH

1 part Corazón reposado tequila
2 parts cranberry juice
2 parts pineapple juice

Shake and serve straight up or on the rocks.

CORAZONADA

1½ parts Corazón de Agave blanco tequila
½ part strawberry liqueur
½ part coconut cream
4 fresh strawberries (plus 1 for garnish)

Muddle fresh strawberries. Serve on the rocks and garnish with a strawberry.

COSMOLITO

1 oz. 1800 silver tequila
½ oz. orange liqueur
2 oz. cranberry juice
½ oz. fresh lime juice
lime wedge for garnish

Shake with ice and strain into a martini glass. Garnish with a lime wedge.

COSMOQUILA

2 oz. Casa Noble tequila crystal or gold
1 oz. Cointreau
¼ oz. fresh lime juice

Shake with ice and strain into a cocktail glass.

COSMORITA

1½ oz. Buen Amigo tequila
½ oz. triple sec
½ oz. fresh lime juice
½ oz. cranberry juice
1 tbsp. agavero liqueur
lime slice for garnish

*Shake or blend first four ingredients. Serve in a chilled cocktail glass.
Float agavero. Garnish with a lime slice.*

COSMOTEQUILA

2 oz. tequila Casa Noble gold
1 oz. Cointreau
½ oz. fresh lime juice
splash cranberry juice

Shake with ice and strain into a cocktail glass.

COUNTRY ROSE

1 oz. Tequila Rose
½ oz. Southern Comfort
½ oz. strawberry schnapps
½ oz. amaretto
3 oz. milk

Mix and pour over ice.

COWBOY KILLER

1¼ oz. tequila
¾ oz. Baileys Irish cream
½ oz. butterscotch schnapps
half-and-half to fill
cherry for garnish

Pour first three ingredients into a cocktail glass. Add ice and fill with half-and-half. Pour into a shaker, shake, and pour back into the glass. Garnish with a cherry.

COWGIRL'S PRAYER

2 oz. tequila
1 oz. fresh lime juice
lemonade to fill
lemon and lime slices for garnish

Stir into a Collins glass over ice cubes. Garnish with slices of lemon and lime.

CRAN RAZZ

2 oz. Buen Amigo tequila
2 oz. cranberry juice
1 oz. raspberry liqueur

In a shaker, mix all ingredients. Serve over rocks.

CRAZY ORGASM

1 oz. tequila
1 oz. vodka
⅓ oz. cranberry juice
⅓ oz. orange juice
pinch sugar

Stir well with ice and strain into a cocktail glass over ice.

CRIPPLE CREEK

½ oz. Buen Amigo tequila
½ oz. Benchmark bourbon
1 oz. orange juice
½ oz. Galliano

Shake first three ingredients and strain into a glass. Float Galliano.

CRYING GAME

1 oz. tequila
⅕ oz. Jack Daniel's whisky
⅕ oz. Absolut vodka
⅕ oz. Kahlua
⅕ oz. Baileys Irish cream
1 oz. rum
⅕ oz. grenadine
5 oz. tomato juice
celery stalk for garnish
green onion for garnish

Mix Jack Daniel's, Absolut vodka, and Kahlua. Heat Baileys Irish cream, tequila, and rum over medium flame. Mix all with tomato juice, and top with grenadine. Garnish with a stalk of celery and a green onion.

CUCARACHA

1 oz. tequila Casa Noble gold
½ oz. Kahlua
½ oz. Cointreau

Combine ingredients in a cocktail glass.

CUERVO AND GINGER

1½ oz. Jose Cuervo Especial tequila
3 oz. ginger ale
lime wedge

Squeeze lime wedge into a glass with ice, add Jose Cuervo Especial, and then add ginger ale. Stir well.

CUERVO CRUSH

1½ oz. Jose Cuervo gold tequila
4 oz. fresh-squeezed orange juice
lime wheel for garnish

Stir in a tall glass with crushed ice. Garnish with a lime wheel.

CUERVO GOLD MARGARITA

1½ oz. Jose Cuervo gold tequila
1 oz. triple sec
2 oz. lime juice
2 oz. sweet and sour mix
lime squeeze
lime wheel for garnish

Blend. Garnish with a lime wheel.

CUERVO MOONLIGHT MARGARITA

1½ oz. Jose Cuervo gold tequila
1 oz. blue curaçao
1 oz. lime juice
lime squeeze
salt to rim glass
lime slice for garnish

Rub rim of cocktail glass with lime rind, dip glass into salt. Blend. Garnish with a lime slice.

CUERVO ORANGE MARGARITA

1½ oz. Jose Cuervo gold tequila
½ oz. triple sec
3 oz. orange juice
½ oz. sweet and sour mix
strawberries for garnish

Blend. Garnish with strawberries.

CUERVO PEACH MARGARITA

1½ oz. Jose Cuervo gold tequila
1 oz. triple sec
1 oz. lime juice
½ cup canned peaches for garnish

Blend. Garnish with peach slices.

CUERVO RASPBERRY MARGARITA

1½ oz. Jose Cuervo gold tequila
1 oz. triple sec
1 oz. lime juice
½ cup frozen raspberries
fresh raspberries for garnish

Blend. Garnish with fresh raspberries.

CUERVO SPIKE

1½ oz. Jose Cuervo gold tequila
grapefruit juice to fill

Pour Jose Cuervo into a glass and fill with grapefruit juice. Stir and serve.

CUERVO STRAWBERRY MARGARITA

1½ oz. Jose Cuervo gold tequila
1 oz. triple sec
1 oz. lime juice
½ cup frozen strawberries
fresh strawberries for garnish

Blend. Garnish with strawberries.

DAGGER

⅓ oz. crème de cacao
⅓ oz. De Kuyper Peachtree schnapps
⅓ oz. Jose Cuervo tequila

Layer.

DAISY

2 oz. tequila
2 tsp. lemon juice
2 tsp. grenadine
2 tsp. club soda

Shake first three ingredients well with ice and strain into a glass with ice. Top with club soda.

DAKOTA

1½ oz. XXX tequila
½ oz. bourbon

Combine in a shot glass.

DANGEROUS LIAISONS

Equal parts:
XXX tequila
Tia Maria
cointreau
splash sour mix

Shake with ice and strain into a chilled cordial glass.

DARING DYLAN

2 oz. tequila
1 oz. Kahlua
4 oz. hot chocolate

Let the hot chocolate cool to room temperature. Pour all of the ingredients into an Irish coffee glass almost filled with crushed ice.

DC

1 oz. XXX tequila
1 oz. Baileys Irish cream

Pour tequila in a double shot glass, then add Baileys.

DEATH AT NIGHT

½ shot tequila
½ shot black sambuca

Layer in a shot glass and serve.

DEATH IN A BOTTLE

1 oz. tequila
1 oz. vodka
1 oz. whisky
1 oz. Bacardi Limon
3 oz. strawberry mix
2 oz. orange juice
2 oz. cranberry juice

Pour into an empty bottle. Shake well and drink.

DECEIVER

2 oz. tequila
½ oz. Galliano

Build in rocks glass with cubed ice. This one will fool you.

DESERT BERRY

1½ oz. Buen Amigo tequila
dash Chambord

Shake with ice and strain into a shot glass.

DEVIL'S BREW

1 shot tequila
½ shot De Kuyper crème de cassis
large dash lime juice
ginger ale
lime slice for garnish

Pour the first four ingredients in a hurricane glass and stir. Top with ginger ale. Garnish with a lime slice.

DIABLO

2 oz. Casa Noble reposado tequila
⅛ oz. crème de cassis
⅛ oz. fresh lime juice
1 oz. ginger ale
lime wedge for garnish

Shake in a mixing glass with ice, then strain into a glass. Garnish with a lime wedge.

DIABLO #2

2 oz. Casa Noble reposado tequila
¼ oz. crème de cassis
½ oz. fresh lime juice
ginger ale to fill
lime wedge for garnish

Build first three ingredients over ice in a Collins glass and fill with ginger ale. Garnish with a lime wedge.

DIRTY ASHTRAY

½ oz. Jose Cuervo tequila
½ oz. vodka
½ oz. pineapple juice
½ oz. grenadine
½ oz. light rum
½ oz. blue curaçao
½ oz. gin
2 oz. sweet and sour mix
lemon wedge for garnish

Shake with ice and pour into a highball glass. Garnish with a lemon wedge.

DISARITA MARGARITA

1 oz. Buen Amigo tequila
½ oz. Disaronno amaretto
3 oz. margarita mix
½ cup crushed Ice
lime slice for garnish

Blend. Garnish with a lime slice.

DISTINGUISHED

1 oz. anejo tequila
½ oz. Grand Marnier
½ oz. lime juice
splash sour mix
splash orange juice
2 cherries for garnish

Shake. Add two flags (cherries). Serve in a martini glass.

DIVA

1½ oz. Oro Azul anejo tequila
½ oz. Cointreau
2 oz. fresh-squeezed lemon juice
1 oz. pear juice
1 oz. simple syrup
lime wedge for garnish

Shake well with ice until blended and pour into a Collins glass. Garnish with a lime wedge.

DJ'S DELIGHT

1¾ oz. Don Julio blanco tequila
¾ oz. melon liqueur
1 oz. pineapple juice

Pour into a rocks glass over ice and stir.

DOCTOR DAWSON

2 oz. tequila
½ oz. lemon juice
1 tsp. superfine sugar
dash bitters
3 oz. club soda

In a shaker half-filled with ice cubes, combine the tequila, lemon juice, sugar, and bitters. Shake well. Strain into a highball glass almost filled with ice cubes. Top with club soda.

DON EDUARDO BANTANGA

2 oz. Don Eduardo anejo tequila
3 oz. cola
½ oz. lime juice
lime wedge for garnish

Build over ice in a glass and serve with a salted rim. Garnish with a lime wedge.

DON JULIO CHAPALA

1¼ oz. Don Julio blanco tequila
¼ oz. triple sec
1 oz. grenadine
2 oz. orange juice
1 oz. lime juice

Shake with ice and pour into a chilled highball glass.

DON QUIXXXOTE

1 oz. XXX tequila
1 oz. Guinness stout

Serve in a tall shot glass.

DONE FOR THE NIGHT

1 oz. Jose Cuervo tequila
1 oz. vodka
1 oz. gin
4 oz. root beer
¼ oz. cream

Pour first four ingredients into a glass and mix. Top with cream.

DORALTO

1½ oz. tequila
½ oz. lemon juice
½ tsp. superfine sugar
dash bitters
4 oz. tonic water
lime wedge for garnish

Shake the first four ingredients with ice and strain into a highball glass almost filled with ice cubes. Top with tonic water and garnish with a lime wedge.

DOS LUNAS REPOSADO TEQUILA MOONRISE

2 oz. Dos Lunas reposado tequila
2 oz. orange juice
⅛ oz. grenadine

DOUBLE GOLD

¾ oz. Jose Cuervo Especial tequila
¾ oz. Goldschlager
½ oz. Galliano

Serve chilled in a shot glass.

DOWN-UNDER

¼ oz. tequila
½ oz. blue curaçao
¼ oz. rum
¼ oz. triple sec
¼ oz. vodka
1½ oz. soda water

Mix over ice in a cocktail glass.

DOWNSHIFT

2 oz. XXX tequila
2 oz. fruit punch
1 oz. lemon-lime soda
rum to top

Start with lemon-lime soda, add tequila and fruit punch. Float rum. Serve straight up or on the rocks.

DOWNSIDER

1½ oz. tequila
½ oz. crème de bananas
½ oz. Galliano
½ oz. light cream
1 tsp. lemon juice
dash bitters
1 tsp. grenadine

Shake well with ice and strain into a cocktail glass.

DR. PEPPER

1½ oz. Reserva del Señor Almendrado tequila
1½ oz. Jack Daniels
Coca-Cola
lime slice for garnish

Pour first two ingredients into a glass and fill with Coke. Add ice and garnish with a lime slice.

DRAGON SMOOCH

½ oz. Jose Cuervo tequila
½ oz. coffee liqueur

Pour coffee liqueur into a shot glass. Add tequila very slowly so that it does not mix.

DURANGO

1½ oz. tequila
2 tbsp. grapefruit juice
1 tsp. almond extract
mint sprigs for garnish
spring water to fill

Shake the first three ingredients well with ice. Strain into a large tumbler; add ice and fill with spring water. Garnish with mint.

DUVALL CRAWL

1½ oz. tequila
1 oz. melon liqueur
1½ oz. orange juice
1 tsp. grenadine
lime slice for garnish
cherry for garnish

Blender with ice until smooth slush. Pour into a chilled champagne glass. Garnish with a lime slice and a cherry.

DYNAMITE

1 oz. reposado tequila
1 oz. blanco tequila
1 oz. Clamato juice
½ tsp. Tabasco
juice of ½ lime
salt to taste

Build in a glass. Mix, add crushed ice, and salt to taste.

EARTHQUAKE

2 oz. tequila
1 tsp. grenadine
2 strawberries
1–2 dashes orange bitters
3 oz. crushed ice
lime slice for garnish
strawberry for garnish

Combine first five ingredients in a blender at high speed for fifteen seconds. Strain and serve straight up. Garnish with a lime slice and a strawberry.

EL BAÑO

2 oz. Olmeca tequila
2 oz. tonic water
3 oz. orange juice
Twix bar for garnish

Mix and serve in a cocktail glass. Garnish with one Twix bar.

EL BESITO

1 oz. Dos Manos 100 percent anejo tequila
2 oz. apricot puree
½ oz. orange flavored liqueur

Serve tall in a highball glass.

EL MAYOR ALE

1½ oz. El Mayor reposado tequila
5 oz. ginger ale
lime wedge for garnish

Serve in a salt-rimmed highball glass over ice. Garnish with a lime wedge.

EL MAYOR DREAMSICLE

½ oz. El Mayor reposado tequila
½ oz. Cointreau
¾ oz. Amarula cream liqueur
1¼ oz. Arrow white crème de cacao
chocolate syrup to rim glass

Shake well with ice. Dip chilled martini glass into chocolate syrup. Strain into the chocolate rimmed chilled martini glass.

EL TORITO

1 oz. Olmeca tequila
½ oz. dark crème de cacao

Serve in an old-fashioned glass with ice. For an after-dinner variation, serve in a snifter glass with no ice.

ELDORADO

2 oz. Patron tequila
1 tbsp. honey
1½ oz. lemon juice
orange slice for garnish

Shake with ice and strain into a Collins glass over ice. Garnish with an orange slice.

ELECTRIC ICE TEA

1 oz. tequila
1½ oz. rum
1½ oz. vodka
1½ oz. gin
1 oz. triple sec
splash blue curaçao
7UP
lemon slice for garnish

Pour into a highball glass and top with 7UP. Garnish with a lemon slice.

ELECTRIC SCREWDRIVER

¾ oz. Jose Cuervo Especial tequila
¾ oz. Smirnoff Red Label vodka
2 oz. orange juice
1 oz. energy drink
orange slice for garnish

Build in a glass half-filled with ice. Garnish with an orange slice.

ELEPHANT MAN

⅓ oz. tequila
⅓ oz. Jack Daniel's whisky
⅓ oz. Bacardi 151 proof rum

Build in a shot glass, making sure to top with the Bacardi 151 proof rum.

ELIMINATOR

1½ oz. Jose Cuervo tequila
1½ oz. Wild Turkey 101
6 oz. orange soda

Mix all ingredients in tall glass. Add more orange soda to taste, if desired.

EN FUEGO

½ oz. Jose Cuervo gold tequila
½ oz. Cointreau
¼ medium sized avocado
¼ fresh lemon, squeezed
¼ fresh lime, squeezed
5 dashes Tabasco green pepper sauce
kosher salt to rim glass
Tabasco to rim glass
cilantro sprig for garnish

Blend the first six ingredients together. Mix kosher salt and Tabasco sauce and rim glass. Pour drink into glass and garnish with roasted red pepper and a sprig of cilantro.

ETERNAL FIRE STORM

2 parts Jose Cuervo tequila
1 part apple juice
2 parts Galliano
1 part strawberry juice

Mix all ingredients in a long glass and add one ice cube.

ETHNIC SUGAR

2 oz. Jose Cuervo tequila
1 oz. Cointreau
1 tsp. Kool-Aid
4 oz. Coca-Cola

Serve in a tall glass with crushed ice.

EXECUTIVE SUNRISE

1½ oz. tequila gold
4 oz. fresh orange juice
2 tsp. crème de cassis

Pour the tequila and the orange juice into a Collins glass almost filled with ice cubes. Stir well. Drop the cassis into the center of the drink.

EXORCIST

2½ oz. tequila
¾ oz. blue curaçao
¾ oz. lime juice
dash Tabasco

Shake with ice and strain into a cocktail glass.

EXOTIC ERIN

1½ oz. tequila
Tuaca
2 oz. orange juice
sugar to rim glass

Shake tequila and orange juice thoroughly and pour into a sugar-rimmed martini glass. Float Tuaca on top.

EXTENDED JAIL SENTENCE

½ oz. Jose Cuervo tequila
½ oz. Southern Comfort
splash pineapple juice
½ oz. Jack Daniel's whisky

Blend with ice cubes.

FENCE JUMPER

½ oz. Jose Cuervo tequila
½ oz. rum
1 tbsp. Tabasco

Pour tequila and rum into shot glass and add Tabasco.

FINALS NIGHT

2 oz. Jose Cuervo tequila
½ oz. lemon juice
4 oz. coffee
½ oz. brown crème de cacao

Pour into a coffee mug half-filled with ice and stir well.

FIRE ALARM

1 part XXX tequila
Tabasco

Pour tequila into a chilled shot glass and top with Tabasco (the hotter the better).

FIRE & ICE

1½ oz. Corazon anejo tequila
5 dashes Tabasco Habanero Sauce
12 fresh cilantro leaves
1½ oz. fresh juice of one lime
½ cup Häagen-Dazs mango sorbet
1 oz. Marie Brizard mango passion liqueur
mango cubes for garnish
lime slices for garnish
habanero peppers for garnish

Blend with a scoop of ice until well blended. Serve in desired glassware with a brochette of mango cubes, and lime slices; add habanero peppers as a garnish.

FIRE BOMB

1 part tequila
1 part Jack Daniel's whisky
1 part vodka
Tabasco to taste

FLAMING BLUE

½ oz. XXX tequila
½ oz. peppermint schnapps
½ oz. Southern Comfort
½ oz. rum

Pour first three ingredients into a shot glass. Layer rum on top and light 5 seconds. Blow out carefully.

FLAMING DR. NO FLAME BUT HOT

1 shot gold tequila
⅛ oz. Tabasco
1 glass pilsner beer

Pour the first two ingredients into a shot glass and immediately drop it inside the beer glass. Drink immediately, all at once.

FLAMINGO-RITA

2 oz. tequila
5 strawberries
4 oz. sweet and sour mix (or to taste)

Blend with ice until frothy and pour into a tacky pink glass with a flamingo stick or straw.

FLATLINER

¾ oz. tequila
½ oz. cognac (preferably Hennessy)
½ oz. vodka
splash Tabasco

Mix first three ingredients with ice and strain into shot glass. Top with Tabasco.

FLYING COW

1 oz. tequila
1 oz. vodka
1 oz. rum
1 oz. brandy
1 oz. Kahlua
1 banana
cream to taste

Blend with ice until smooth and pour into a highball glass.

FLYING SQUIRREL

1½ oz. Jose Cuervo Especial gold tequila
1 oz. triple sec
splash sweet and sour mix
dash sweetened Rose's lime juice
orange juice to fill

Pour tequila and triple sec into a highball glass one-third filled with crushed ice. Add sour mix and lime juice. Fill with orange juice and serve.

FOUR HORSEMEN

¾ oz. XXX tequila
¾ oz. Jagermeister
¾ oz. Rumpleminze
¾ oz. rum

Shake well with ice and serve in cocktail glass.

FRANCE MEETS MEXICO

1 oz. tequila
1 oz. Chartreuse

Mix both in a rocks glass.

FREDDY FUDPUCKER

2 oz. tequila
4 oz. orange juice
½ oz. Galliano

Pour the first two ingredients into a highball glass almost filled with ice cubes. Pouring slowly and carefully over the back of a teaspoon; float the Galliano on top of the drink.

FREDDY FUDPUCKER II

1 oz. Buen Amigo tequila
4 oz. orange juice
½ oz. Galliano
½ oz. Kahlua

Shake first three ingredients and serve. Layer Kahlua on top.

FRENCHI

1 oz. tequila
1 oz. Midori
1 oz. peach schnapps
passion fruit juice
pineapple wedge for garnish

Pour first three ingredients in a tall glass over ice and fill with passion fruit juice. Garnish with a pineapple wedge.

FROG IN A BLENDER

½ oz. Jose Cuervo tequila
1 tsp. sweet vermouth
½ oz. sloe gin
maraschino cherry for garnish
lime wedge for garnish

Shake well with ice and strain into a tumbler half-filled with crushed ice. Garnish with a maraschino cherry and a lime wedge.

FROGGY POTION

1 oz. Jose Cuervo tequila
1 oz. vodka
1 oz. rum
1 oz. gin
dash Coca-Cola
orange juice to fill

Pour first five ingredients into a glass with ice and fill with orange juice.

FROGSTER

1 oz. Jose Cuervo tequila
½ oz. blue curaçao
orange juice to fill

Build first two ingredients in a highball glass with ice, and finally, for that yummy green color, fill with orange juice.

FROSTBITE

2 oz. Jose Cuervo tequila
1 oz. Mountain Dew
¼ gal. lime sherbet

Blend, carefully.

FROZEN APPLE TART MARGARITA

2 oz. tequila
1 oz. sour apple liqueur
2 oz. sour mix
2–3 drops Tabasco habanero sauce
¼ tsp. sugar
1 cup ice

Blend until smooth.

FROZEN BANANA MARGARITA

1 oz. tequila
¾ oz. banana schnapps
banana
1 tsp. sugar
⅛ tsp. Tabasco habanero sauce
1 cup ice

Blend until smooth.

FROZEN CHOCOLATE BANANA MARGARITA

1½ oz. tequila
1 oz. crème de cacao
banana
1 tsp. chocolate syrup
¼ tsp. Tabasco
1 cup ice

Blend until smooth.

FROZEN GRINGO

1 oz. agavero tequila
1 oz. 1800 reposado tequila
1 oz. lime juice
1 oz. strawberry liqueur
1 cup ice cubes
1 fresh strawberry for garnish

Blend until frothy. Pour the blend into a chilled margarita glass and garnish with a fresh strawberry.

FROZEN MARGARITA WITH JALAPEÑO

1½ oz. tequila
1 oz. Cointreau
4 oz. sour mix
½ oz. lemon juice
1 tbsp. Tabasco green pepper sauce
1 cup ice

Blend until smooth.

FROZEN MATADOR

2½ oz. tequila
2 oz. pineapple juice
1 tbsp. lime juice

Blend briefly with 1 cup crushed ice in an electric blender at low speed.
Pour into an old-fashioned glass and garnish with a pineapple stick.

FROZEN PINA MARGARITA

1½ oz. tequila
1 oz. Cointreau
¼ tsp. Tabasco habanero sauce
6 oz. passion fruit/guava juice
2 tsp. Coco Lopez
1 cup ice

Blend until smooth.

FROZEN SUMMER MELON MARGARITA

1½ oz. tequila
½ oz. Cointreau
1 oz. Midori liqueur
½ oz. lime juice
2–3 drops of Tabasco habanero sauce
1 cup ice

Blend until smooth.

FROZEN TEQUILA SCREWDRIVER

2 oz. tequila
½ oz. Cointreau
3 oz. orange juice
orange slice for garnish

Frappé in a highball glass. Garnish with an orange slice.

FRUITS OF THE DESERT

1½ oz. gold tequila
½ oz. Cointreau
2 oz. grapefruit juice
1 tsp. caster sugar
cherry for garnish

Shake and strain into an old fashioned glass half-filled with broken ice. Garnish with a cherry, and serve.

THE FULL YARD

1 oz. tequila
½ oz. blue curaçao
2 oz. strawberry mix
2 oz. cranberry juice
lots of grenadine

Blend with ice.

FUZZY RITA

1½ oz. Buen Amigo tequila
½ oz. peach liqueur
½ oz. Cointreau
1½ oz. lime juice

Serve on the rocks.

GAIRA POP

2½ oz. Jose Cuervo tequila
1 oz. rum
1½ oz. vodka
½ oz. orange juice
½ oz. lemon juice

Mix the first three ingredients, then add the orange and lemon juice.

GARTER BELT

1 oz. Patron XO Café
1 oz. white crème de cacao
1 oz. heavy cream
finely ground espresso and chocolate for garnish

Shake first three ingredients with ice until well blended. Strain into a chilled cocktail glass. Garnish with a sprinkle of ground espresso and chocolate.

GASOLINE

1½ oz. Southern Comfort
1½ oz. tequila

Build in a lowball glass over ice.

GATES OF HELL

1½ oz. tequila
2 tsp. lemon juice
2 tsp. lime juice
1 tsp. cherry brandy

Shake the first three ingredients well with ice. Strain into an old-fashioned glass almost filled with crushed ice. Drizzle the cherry brandy over the top.

GENERATION X

1 oz. Jose Cuervo tequila
1 oz. triple sec
1 oz. blue curaçao
1 Zima
1 oz. melon liqueur
1 oz. Jim Beam

GENTLE BEN

1 oz. tequila
1 oz. vodka
1 oz. gin
orange juice to fill
orange slice for garnish
cherry for garnish

Shake and pour into a Collins glass over ice cubes. Fill with orange juice and stir. Garnish with an orange slice and a cherry.

GENTLE BULL

1½ oz. Buen Amigo tequila
1 oz. heavy cream
¾ oz. coffee liqueur
1 scoop crushed ice
whipped cream for garnish
cherry for garnish

Shake. Garnish with whipped cream and a cherry.

GEORGIA PEACH MARGARITA

1½ oz. Patron reposado tequila
½ oz. Patron Citronge
splash peach schnapps
½ cup peach sorbet
⅛ oz. lime juice
peach-flavored sugar to rim glass
fresh peach slices for garnish

Blend with a few ice cubes. Rim glass with peach-flavored sugar. Garnish with fresh peach slices.

GEORGIAN SUNRISE

¾ oz. tequila
¼ oz. peach schnapps
½ oz. strawberry liqueur
3 oz. sweet and sour mix
lime slice for garnish

Blend and serve in a highball glass. Garnish with a lime slice.

THE GIRAFFE

2 oz. tequila
½ oz. St. Germain
3 oz. grapefruit juice
2 ice cubes

Pour the first two ingredients into a tall glass, followed by the two ice cubes. Swirl the two around in the glass for a time (note: do not stir), and then add grapefruit juice.

GOLD DRIVER

2 oz. Jose Cuervo tequila
½ oz. Goldschläger
2 oz. orange juice
1 lime slice

Pour the first two ingredients into a short glass over ice. Top with orange juice. Squeeze in the juice from one lime slice.

GOLD STANDARD

2 oz. Cuervo tequila (preferably 1800 Cuervo)
1 oz. Licor 43
½ oz. curaçao
½ oz. sour mix
dash orange juice

Shake and serve in a chilled glass.

GOLDEN SHOWER

½ oz. gold tequila
½ oz. Southern Comfort
2 oz. apple juice
½ oz. Galliano
lemonade to fill

Mix first three ingredients in a mixing tin, then pour over ice in a Collins glass. Top with lemonade and float Galliano.

GRAND MARGARITA

1 oz. Buen Amigo tequila
¾ oz. Grand Marnier
fresh lime juice to taste
sugar to taste
lime wedge for garnish

Pour first two ingredients into a martini glass over ice. Fill with fresh lime juice and sugar to taste. Shake. Garnish with a lime wedge.

GRAPE APE

½ oz. tequila
4 oz. grape juice (white)
white grape for garnish

Shake with ice and pour into a highball glass over ice. Garnish with a white grape.

GRAVEYARD

½ oz. Jose Cuervo tequila
½ oz. Smirnoff vodka
½ oz. gin
½ oz. bourbon
½ oz. scotch
½ oz. triple sec
½ oz. 151 rum
Equal parts:
beer
stout

Pour first seven ingredients into a beer mug. Fill with half beer and half stout.

GREEN APPLE TEQUINI

2 oz. Casa Noble Crystal tequila (silver)
1 oz. apple schnapps
splash Midori
lime squeeze
green apple slice for garnish

Shake with ice and strain into a cocktail glass. Garnish with a slice of green apple.

GREEN ARROW

1 part gold tequila
1 oz. lemon juice
½ oz. lime juice
1 part blue curaçao
½ oz. crushed ice

Mix in a jar, then stir to obtain the green color.

GREEN DINOSAUR

1½ oz. white tequila
1½ oz. Midori
1½ oz. gin
1½ oz. vodka
1½ oz. rum
1½ oz. triple sec
3⅓ oz. sweet and sour mix
Sprite

Pour first seven ingredients into a glass over ice, fill with Sprite, and mix.

THE GREEN HORNITO

2 limes
2 oz. Sauza reposado hornitos tequila
½ oz. Cointreau
4–5 small sprigs cilantro
⅛ tsp. Tabasco green pepper sauce
lime slice for garnish

Juice limes using a reamer and pour juice into a shaker. Add in ½ a lime (to extract the essence when muddling). Add remaining ingredients. Muddle well and strain into a chilled martini glass. Garnish with a lime slice.

GREEN LIZARD

1 oz. tequila
½ oz. St. Germain
½ oz. green crème de menthe

A weaker tequila drink for the beginner tequila drinkers.

GREEN MEXICAN

1 oz. tequila
1 oz. Midori
sour mix to fill
orange slice for garnish
cherry for garnish

Pour first two ingredients into a Collins glass over ice. Fill with sour mix and garnish with an orange slice and a cherry.

GREEN THUNDER

1 oz. Jose Cuervo tequila
1 oz. vodka
6 oz. lemon juice
⅓ oz. sugar

Shake; serve in a tall glass.

GREEN ZONE

2 oz. XXX tequila
1 oz. Pisang Ambon
4 oz. orange juice
lime slice for garnish

Blend with ice and serve in a highball glass. Garnish with a lime slice.

GRIMOSA

2 oz. Jose Cuervo tequila
2 oz. orange juice
4 oz. champagne

Serve in a chilled champagne flute.

GTV

1 oz. Jose Cuervo tequila
1 oz. vodka
½ oz. gin

The ingredients are best preserved cold for this purpose. To mix, pour the ingredients into a glass. Add an ice cube, if you like.

GUADALAJARA SUNRISE

½ oz. XXX tequila
½ oz. peach schnapps
½ oz. strawberry liqueur
3 oz. sweet and sour mix
lime slice for garnish

Blend with ice and serve in a highball glass. Garnish with a lime slice.

HAIR OF THE DOG

½ oz. tequila
½ oz. Irish whisky
¼ oz. Tabasco
¼ oz. salt

Pour first three ingredients into a shot glass. Lay salt on top. Dance.

HAIRY SUNRISE

¾ oz. tequila
¾ oz. vodka
½ oz. Cointreau
3 oz. orange juice
3 dashes grenadine
lime slice for garnish

Blend first four ingredients and pour into a Collins glass. Float grenadine and garnish with a lime slice.

HARLEM MUGGER

½ oz. Jose Cuervo tequila
½ oz. vodka
3 oz. champagne
lime wedge
½ oz. Bacardi Light rum
½ oz. gin
cranberry juice

Build over ice.

HARRISON SPECIAL

2 oz. Jose Cuervo tequila
2 oz. vodka
2 oz. rum
3 oz. Cointreau
2 oz. gin
dash Coca-Cola

Pour first five ingredients into a glass over ice. Top with Coca-Cola (for color). Stir and serve.

HARSH

1½ oz. Jagermeister
1½ oz. tequila
dash Tabasco garlic sauce

Mix and serve in a shot glass.

HAWAIIAN SEDUCTION

1 oz. tequila
1 oz. vodka
1 oz. lime juice

Pour first two ingredients into a tall glass and fill with lime juice. Add ice and mix very well.

HEAD BLOWER

1 oz. tequila
1 oz. whisky
½ oz. dark rum
½ glass super strong beer
½ tsp. black pepper

Serve in a chilled beer mug.

HEADCRUSH

2 oz. Jose Cuervo tequila
whipped cream to top
½ oz. Tabasco green pepper sauce
salt

Pour tequila into a glass, and then add Tabasco sauce carefully. Put on a top with whipped cream and add some salt.

HEAVEN

½ part tequila
⅓ part vodka
⅓ part Cointreau
⅓ part pink lemonade

Pour into a large glass over crushed ice.

HEAVEN AND EARTH

1 oz. tequila
½ oz. vodka
½ oz. white rum
¼ oz. gin
½ oz. peach schnapps

Blend with crushed ice. Serve with a soda back.

HEAVENLY BILLIONAIRE'S MARGARITA

2 oz. Gran Centenario anejo tequila
1 oz. Gran Marnier Cuvee du Cent Cinquantenaire
1½ oz. fresh-squeezed lime juice
½ orange wheel for garnish

Shake vigorously with ice and strain into a prechilled martini glass. Garnish with half an orange wheel.

HEAVENLY HIGHBALL

1½ oz. Gran Centenario Plata tequila
1½ oz. cranberry juice
3 oz. ginger ale
several mint leaves and a mint sprig
½ oz. fresh lime juice

Muddle the mint leaves with the cranberry juice in the bottom of a high-ball glass. Add ice. Build the rest of the ingredients and stir. Garnish with a mint sprig.

HELL MARY

1½ oz. Pecos Heat chili pepper tequila
dash bitters
dash Tabasco
dash horseradish
1 oz. Aalborg Akvavit
V-8 juice
celery stalk for garnish
lemon wedge for garnish

Pour first five ingredients into a glass, fill with V-8, and shake vigorously. Add black pepper to taste and garnish with a celery stalk and lemon wedge. Serve in a Collins glass with ice.

HIGH VOLTAGE

6 parts Jose Cuervo tequila
1 part lime juice
3 parts peach liqueur

Shake and serve in a chilled glass.

HINA BLAST

4 oz. tequila
6 oz. red wine
1 oz. Coca-Cola
3 oz. orange juice
3 tbsp. bananas (chopped)
1 cup raisins
6 oz. Dom Perignon
¼ tsp. red pepper (hot and in flakes)

Heat wine, add raisins, and boil. Mix Coca-Cola, tequila, and orange juice and add to mixture. Toss bananas with hot red pepper flakes. Pour Dom Perignon over bananas. Mix everything together and store in a glass jar. Chill overnight. Have lots of money!

HOLE IN ONE

1 part tequila
1 part scotch
1 part vodka
1 part Cointreau

Stir, then add crushed ice.

HOLLYWOOD TEA

½ oz. Jose Cuervo tequila
½ oz. vodka
½ oz. light rum
½ oz. gin
7UP

Shake first four ingredients with ice and strain into ice-filled glass. Fill with 7UP.

HONOLULU ACTION

1 part vodka
1 part grenadine
1 part blue curaçao
1 part Bacardi 151
1 part Baileys Irish cream
1 part Midori
1 part Jose Cuervo tequila
whipped cream
Li Hing powder for sprinkling

Layer ingredients in the above order, top with whipped cream, then top with a sprinkle of Li Hing powder.

HOO HOO

1½ oz. tequila
1½ oz. Midori
½ oz. grenadine
melon ball for garnish (optional)

Shake with ice and strain into a martini glass. Garnish with a small melon ball if desired.

HORSESHOE

2 oz. Jose Cuervo tequila
1 oz. Southern Comfort
8 oz. orange juice
2 dashes grenadine
1 oz. bourbon

Cover the bottom of the glass with one dash of grenadine. Pour in the tequila followed by the bourbon and finally the Southern Comfort. Flood the glass with the orange juice. Pour in the remaining grenadine.

HOT APPLE ROSE

2 oz. Tequila Rose
apple cider to fill
whipped cream for garnish

Pour tequila into a mug and fill with hot apple cider. Garnish with whipped cream.

HOT BOMB

1¾ oz. Buen Amigo tequila
¼ oz. Du Bouchett hot cinnamon schnapps
2 dashes Tabasco

Shake with ice and strain into shot glass.

HOT CHA CHA MARTINI

2 oz. 1800 tequila
1 oz. Tuaca
2 oz. fresh lemon juice
dash Tabasco habanero sauce
2 dashes Tabasco green pepper sauce
jalapeño-stuffed olives for garnish

Chill a 6 oz. martini glass and salt rim. Shake well and strain into the martini glass. Garnish with jalapeño-stuffed olives.

HOT CHOCOLATE ROSE

1½ oz. Tequila Rose
hot chocolate to fill

Pour Tequila Rose into a mug and fill with hot chocolate.

HOT KISS

1½ oz. Partida silver tequila
¾ oz. Berentzen apple schnapps
1 oz. unfiltered apple juice
½ oz. fresh-squeezed lime juice
½ oz. agave nectar or simple syrup
¼ oz. Tabasco
red chili pepper for garnish

Shake with ice and strain into a chilled cocktail glass. Garnish with a red chili pepper.

HOT MELONS

1½ oz. Patron silver tequila
3 oz. Red Bull Energy Drink
½ oz. melon liqueur
½ oz. fresh mango
1 maraschino cherry
8 dashes Tabasco green pepper sauce
cucumber spear for garnish

Muddle mango, cherry, and Tabasco together. Add tequila, melon liqueur, and Red Bull. Shake and strain into a chilled martini glass. Garnish with a long-ways sliced cucumber spear and skewer a peperoncini pepper to it.

HOT PANTS

2 oz. tequila
½ oz. peppermint schnapps
1 tbsp. fresh grapefruit juice
1 tsp. superfine sugar or simple syrup
lime to rim glass
salt to rim glass
lime wedge for garnish

Rim an old-fashioned glass with lime and salt, and chill briefly. Shake with ice, then strain into a glass over ice. Garnish with a lime wedge.

HOT SHOT

1½ oz. Jose Cuervo tequila
boiling water
1 beef bouillon cube
salt and pepper

Dissolve the cube of beef bouillon in a mug of boiling water. Add the tequila and season to taste.

HOT "T"

2 oz. Tarantula reposado tequila
3 dashes Tabasco chipotle pepper sauce

Serve in a shot glass.

HOT TO TROT

½ oz. Jose Cuervo tequila
½ oz. De Kuyper Hot Damn cinnamon schnapps
dash lime juice

Rim a shooter glass with lime and salt and pour the first two ingredients in. Add a dash of lime juice and SLAM!

HOT TODDY

4 oz. XXX tequila
2 oz. apple cider
8 oz. cranberry juice cocktail
2 oz. orange liqueur

In a saucepan, heat cider and cranberry juice cocktail just until hot (do not let boil) and remove from heat. Stir in tequila and orange liqueur. Serve toddies in mugs, garnished with lime slices.

HOTTIE

2 oz. Patron tequila
1 tbsp. dark chocolate (Hershey's), melted
2 oz. milk
Tabasco habanero pepper sauce
½ oz. Grand Marnier
cherry for garnish

Shake the first four ingredients with ice and pour into a cognac glass. Or, heat the first four ingredients in the microwave and pour into a cognac glass for a warm drink. Float the Grand Marnier and garnish with a cherry.

HUEVOS BUSTER

1½ oz. Reserva del Señor Almendrado tequila
1½ oz. light rum
Coke or Diet Coke

Pour first two ingredients into a glass and fill with Coke.

HUG IT OUT MARGARITA

2 parts Sauza Commemorativo tequila
1 tbsp. fresh pomegranate juice
1 part De Kuyper triple sec
2 parts fresh-squeezed lime juice
lime slice for garnish

Shake over ice. Serve in a margarita glass and garnish with a lime slice.

HURRICANE FLINT

1 oz. Jose Cuervo tequila
2 tsp. lime juice
1 tbsp. passion fruit concentrate
1 oz. Malibu coconut rum

Shake with ice and strain into a cocktail glass.

HURRICANE LEAH

¼ oz. tequila
¼ oz. white rum
¼ oz. gin
¼ oz. vodka
¼ oz. blue curaçao
dash cherry brandy
3 oz. sour mix
3 oz. orange juice
orange wheel for garnish

Build in a parfait glass and stir. Garnish with an orange wheel.

I AM FINE

1½ oz. tequila
½ oz. white rum
8 drops Tabasco
salt and pepper
Sprite

Pour first three ingredients into a glass and top with Sprite. Add salt and pepper to taste. Mix.

ICE BET

1½ oz. tequila
¼ oz. Cointreau
dash Tabasco green pepper sauce

Serve with ice in a brandy glass.

ICEBREAKER

2 oz. Tezón tequila
2 oz. grapefruit juice
1 tbsp. grenadine
½ oz. triple sec

Mix with ice and strain into a sour glass.

IDIOT

1½ oz. tequila
1 oz. Tampico Citrus Punch

Pour into a cocktail glass and stir.

IGUANA

1½ oz. Buen Amigo tequila
¾ oz. Nikolai vodka
¾ oz. coffee liqueur

Serve on the rocks.

INCOGNITO

1½ oz. Jose Cuervo Clásico tequila
¾ oz. apricot brandy
3 dashes bitters
¼ oz. lime juice

Shake well with ice.

ILANA STERN ICE

3 parts tequila
1 part ice tea

Just pour, give a moment of silence as homage to the gods, and then down it and serve another.

INOCULATION SHOT

1¾ oz. Jose Cuervo gold tequila
¼ oz. blue curaçao
splash Tabasco sweet & spicy pepper sauce

Combine in a shot glass.

INVISIBLE HOMBRE

1½ parts Corazon tequila blanco
2½ parts tonic water
splash lime
lime twist for garnish

Garnish with a lime twist.

IRONMAN

1 part Jose Cuervo tequila
1 part sambuca
1 part green Chartreuse
3 parts Tabasco
1 part scotch

Mix in a shot glass.

JACKHAMMER

½ oz. tequila
½ oz. Jack Daniel's

Pour into shot glass.

JADE MONKEY

1 oz. Jose Cuervo tequila
¼ oz. lime juice
1 tsp. vanilla extract
2 oz. Kool-Aid

JALAPEÑO

1 oz. Tabasco green pepper sauce
2 oz. tequila 100 percent agave blanco
1 chunk mango, peeled
½ oz. Tabasco green pepper sauce
2 oz. tequila 100 percent agave blanco
1½ oz. lime juice
1½ oz. mango juice
1 chunk mango, peeled

Shake first three ingredients with ice, strain. Add the next four ingredients, shake with ice, strain, and add mango.

JELL-O MARGARITA

4 oz. Jose Cuervo Especial gold tequila
4 oz. Finest Call margarita mix
8 oz. boiling water
1 package Jello
1 slice lime

Combine boiling water and contents of Jello package in medium sized saucepan. Stir until completely dissolved. Instead of using 1 cup cold water use 4 oz. (½ cup) tequila and 4 oz. (½ cup) margarita mix. Pour into a margarita glass. Garnish with a piece of lime set inside mixture. Chill until set. Makes 3 cocktails.

Note: if salt is desired, make sure to rim the glass before pouring mixture.

JELLYBEAN

splash grenadine
½ oz. sambuca
½ oz. Jose Cuervo tequila

Layer.

JELLYFISH

½ oz. tequila, white
½ oz. sambuca, white
drop Tabasco

Pour first two ingredients into a shot glass and top with 1 drop of Tabasco.

JOHAN'S SCREAM

2 oz. gold tequila
2 lime wedges
2 tsp. brown sugar
2 orange wedges
5 mint leaves

Serve on the rocks.

JOKER'S TEA

½ oz. tequila
½ oz. vodka
½ oz. rum
½ oz. Jim Beam
½ oz. blue curaçao
⅓ part sweet and sour mix
⅔ part Coca-Cola
lime wedge for garnish

Pour first five ingredients into a glass and fill with sweet and sour mix and Coke. Shake and garnish with a lime wedge.

JUKEBOX RANDY

1½ oz. Jose Cuervo tequila
½ oz. whisky

Serve as a shot.

JUMPING BEAN

1½ oz. Jose Cuervo tequila
½ oz. sambuca
3 coffee beans

Shake first two ingredients with ice and strain drink into a cocktail glass. Drop coffee beans into middle of drink, and serve.

JUNGLE SLUT

1 oz. tequila
1 oz. green Chartreuse
splash Tabasco garlic sauce

Serve straight up in a shot glass.

KANSAS CITY SLUDGE

2 oz. tequila
1 oz. vodka
1 oz. bitters
1½ oz. maple syrup

Build (in order) in a glass.

KERMIT'S REVENGE

1 oz. tequila
1 oz. vodka
1 oz. rum
1 oz. triple sec
1 oz. crème de menthe
1 oz. gin
lemonade to fill

Mix first six ingredients in a jug and fill with lemonade and ice. Serves 3.

KEY LIME TINI

1 oz. El Mayor reposado tequila
½ oz. KeKe Beach key lime liqueur
½ oz. Tuaca
½ oz. Rose's lime juice
½ oz. cream

Shake well with ice and strain into chilled martini glass.

KILL ME NOW

1 oz. tequila
1 oz. vodka
1 oz. amaretto
½ oz. 151 proof rum
½ oz. gin

Mix in a hurricane glass over crushed ice.

KNOCKOUT PUNCH

1 shot rum
1 shot tequila
8 oz. fruit punch

Serve in a very tall glass.

L.A.P.D. NIGHTSHIFT

1 part tequila
1 part grenadine
1 part blue curaçao

Layer in a shot glass.

LA BAMBA

1½ oz. tequila
½ oz. Cointreau
1½ oz. pineapple juice
1½ oz. orange juice
splash grenadine

Shake well with ice and strain into a cocktail glass.

LA HABANA

2 oz. XXX tequila
2 oz. apricot brandy
few drops lime juice

Pour the first two ingredients into a cocktail shaker half full with ice cubes. Add lime juice. Shake well. Strain into a martini glass over ice cubes.

LA JOLLARITA

1½ oz. Buen Amigo tequila
½ oz. Cointreau
½ oz. Chambord

Shake with ice and strain into a glass.

LA PALOMA

1½ oz. Zapopan silver tequila
½ oz. fresh lime juice
grapefruit soda (not juice)

Pour first two ingredients into a highball glass over ice and fill with grapefruit soda.

LA PALOMA SUPREMA

1½ oz. Don Julio reposado tequila
4 oz. grapefruit soda
salt to rim glass
lime wedge for garnish

Pour into a salt-rimmed, ice-filled highball glass. Garnish with a lime wedge.

LADIES NIGHT

1 oz. Patron XO Café
1 oz. Stoli vanilla
1 oz. amaretto or Frangelico
coffee beans for garnish

Shake well with ice and strain into a chilled martini glass. Garnish with coffee beans.

LAKEWATER

2 shots vodka
4 shots blueberry schnapps
2 shots Jack Daniel's
2 shots tequila
2 shots gin
Coca-Cola

Mix first five ingredients in a large pitcher and fill with Coca-Cola. Serves 4 people.

LATIN LOVER

1½ oz. tequila
¾ oz. amaretto

Pour into an old-fashioned glass and fill with ice.

LAZER BEAM

½ oz. tequila
½ oz. Southern Comfort
½ oz. vodka
½ oz. lime juice
½ oz. amaretto
1 oz. triple sec
½ oz. sloe gin
orange juice to fill (optional)

Mix first seven ingredients and pour over ice in a tall glass. Orange juice may be added to fill.

LAZY SUNDAY

2 oz. tequila
1 oz. ginger ale
2½ oz. cranberry juice
lime wedge for garnish

Serve in a tall glass with ice. Garnish with a lime wedge.

LEMONADE

1 oz. Buen Amigo tequila
1 oz. orange curaçao
1 oz. club soda
1 oz. cranberry juice
juice of ½ lemon
lemon wedge for garnish

Garnish with a lemon wedge.

LIFE IN HELL

1 oz. tequila
dash Everclear
⅓ oz. Tabasco
1 jalapeño pepper slice

Layer Tabasco and tequila in a shot glass. Drop in jalapeño. Top off with Everclear.

LIQUID VALIUM

⅔ oz. tequila
⅔ oz. amaretto
⅔ oz. triple sec
⅔ Jack Daniel's

Serve in a shooter glass.

LIZARD'S SLIME

1½ oz. Buen Amigo tequila
Midori melon liqueur to float

Pour tequila into a shot glass, and float Midori.

LOCO LEMONADE

1½ oz. tequila
1 oz. grenadine
4 oz. lemonade
½ oz. lemon juice

Build over ice and squeeze lemon juice over to top.

LOLITA

2 oz. tequila
⅓ oz. lime juice
1 tsp. honey
2 dashes Angostura bitters

Shake and strain over one or two ice cubes in a cocktail glass.

LONG BEACH

1 part tequila
1 part vodka
1 part rum
2 parts sour mix
1 part gin
cranberry juice to fill
lemon slice for garnish

Pour equal amounts of liquor to approximately half the glass. Pour sour mix to ¾ point of glass. Fill with cranberry juice. Garnish with a lemon slice.

LONG ISLAND ICE TEA

¼ oz. tequila
¼ oz. gin
¼ oz. whisky
¼ oz. white rum
¼ oz. vodka
1 oz. simple syrup
splash Coca-Cola
orange juice to fill

Mix alcohol in large glass, add syrup, and fill with orange juice. Add a splash of Coca-Cola for color.

LONG WALK OFF A SHORT PIER

½ oz. tequila
½ oz. Bacardi 151 proof rum
½ oz. bourbon whisky
½ oz. vodka
½ oz. gin
½ oz. Irish whisky
½ oz. Midori
Coca-Cola

Pour first seven ingredients over ice in a highball glass. Fill with Coca-Cola.

LOS ALTOS

1 oz. Oro Azul anejo tequila
½ oz. coffee liqueur
¾ oz. hazelnut liqueur
1 oz. whipping cream flavored with green crème de menthe

LOUDMOUTH

1 oz. tequila
1 oz. Kahlua
3 oz. cranberry juice

Shake well with ice and strain into a Collins glass over ice.

LOVE IMPOSSIBLE

¼ oz. tequila
½ oz. vodka
½ oz. vermouth
¼ oz. gin
¼ oz. Kahlua
1 oz. cream

Blend and pour into a Collins glass.

LOVE POTION

1½ oz. tequila
2 tbsp. grenadine
1½ oz. triple sec
1½ oz. blackberry brandy
4 oz. lemon mix

Shake with ice. Serve over ice in a tall glass.

LOVER'S MARGARITA

1 oz. agavero tequila
1 oz. 1800 reposado tequila
splash fresh lime juice
lime wedge for garnish

Pour over ice, garnish with a lime wedge. Salt rim if you prefer. We recommend doubling the recipe and using two straws.

THE LUBRICATOR TM

1½ oz. XXX tequila
1 oz. orange liquor
juice of ½ lemon
juice of ½ lime
splash cranberry juice

Serve on the rocks or shake vigorously with cracked ice in a stainless steel shaker and strain into a broad-bowled, stemmed cocktail glass.

MACARENA

1 oz. Buen Amigo tequila
½ oz. Malibu coconut rum
3 oz. sweet and sour mix
1 oz. orange juice
1 oz. pineapple juice
splash cranberry juice
pineapple slice for garnish
orange slice for garnish
cherry for garnish

Shake and pour over ice into a 1 oz. tumbler. Garnish with a pineapple slice, an orange slice, and a cherry.

MACHISMO

1 shot agavero tequila
1 slice lime
sugar

Coat a lime slice with sugar. After you drink the shot, lick lime with sugar.

MADRAS

1½ oz. 1800 reposado tequila
2 oz. cranberry juice
1 oz. orange juice
dash lime juice
orange slice for garnish

Shake over ice or blend. Garnish with an orange slice.

MAGIC

1 oz. tequila
1 oz. vodka
1 oz. triple sec
1 oz. Bacardi light rum
1 oz. gin
cola syrup

Mix first five ingredients over crushed ice and top with cola syrup.

MAGIC MOJO MIX

32 oz. fruit punch
1 fifth tequila
1 fifth vodka
2 oz. Kahlua
2 oz. lime juice
splash Mountain Dew

Mix in a large container. Stir until all the sugar dissolves and store in a dark cool place for seven days. Serve with Mountain Dew in the bottom half of the glass.

MALCOLM LOWRY

1 oz. mezcal
1 scoop crushed ice
¾ oz. lemon or lime juice
¾ oz. Cointreau
¾ oz. white rum

Mix with crushed ice and strain into an iced cocktail glass with a salted rim.

MALIBU WAVE

1 oz. tequila
½ oz. triple sec
⅛ oz. blue curaçao
1½ oz. sweet and sour mix
lime slice for garnish

Shake with ice and strain into a chilled cocktail glass. Garnish with a slice of lime.

MAMA CALIENTE

1½ oz. Corazon anejo tequila
4 dashes of Tabasco Chipotle Pepper Sauce
½ oz. Trader Vic's rock candy syrup
1½ oz. fresh lime juice
¾ oz. passion fruit coulis
1 oz. Cointreau

Shake well with ice and strain into a glass.

MARGAMIGO

2 oz. Buen Amigo tequila
1 oz. fresh lime juice
dash Stolichnaya orange
coarse salt to rim glass
lime juice to rim glass
lime wedge for garnish

Shake or blend and strain into a chilled cocktail glass, the rim of witch has been moistened with lime juice and dipped in salt. Garnish with a lime wedge.

MARGARITA MADRES

1¼ oz. Buen Amigo tequila
½ oz. Cointreau
1½ oz. sweet and sour mix
1½ oz. orange juice
1½ oz. cranberry juice

Blend.

MARVELOUS PEACH

1½ oz. XXX tequila
2 oz. peach juice
2 oz. pineapple juice
lime slice for garnish

Pour ingredients into a highball glass over ice. Mix and garnish with a lime slice.

MASSACRE

2 oz. tequila
1 tsp. Campari
4 oz. ginger ale

Pour the first two ingredients into a highball glass over ice and top with ginger ale. Stir well.

MAXIMUM MARTINI

1½ oz. Pepe Lopez gold tequila
splash extra dry vermouth
3 drops vanilla extract

Shake vigorously and strain into a chilled martini glass.

MAYAN

2 oz. Buen Amigo tequila
3 oz. orange juice
7UP
lime wedge for garnish

Pour first two ingredients into a glass and fill with 7UP. Garnish with a lime wedge.

MC RITA

2 oz. tequila
2 oz. Cointreau
2 oz. sweet and sour mix
2 oz. Rose's lime juice
salt to rim glass
lime wedge for garnish

Pulse with ice in a blender. Pour into a glass rimmed with salt and garnish with a lime wedge. Serves.

THE MCILHENY SWAMP RITA

1 shot tequila (Centario)
2 oz. margarita mix (South of the Border)
1 splash of triple sec
1 splash of sweet and sour mix
1 Tab energy drink
2 dashes Tabasco

Combine first four ingredients in glass with ice. Top with Tab energy drink and finish with Tabasco sauce.

MELON MARGARITA

1 oz. Two Fingers tequila
1 oz. melon liqueur
1½ oz. sweet and sour
½ oz. triple sec
lime wedge for garnish

Shake and strain into a chilled cocktail glass. Garnish with a lime wedge.

MELONELLO MARGARITA

1 oz. Two Fingers tequila
1 oz. melon liqueur
1 oz. Caravella Lemoncello
1½ oz. sweet and sour
½ oz. triple sec

Shake and strain into a chilled cocktail glass. Garnish with a lime wedge.

MENTA

2 parts Corazón reposado tequila
6-8 mint leaves
2–3 dashes bitters

Muddle mint leaves in base of shaker, then add all other ingredients. Shake with ice.

MERLIN

1¾ oz. Buen Amigo tequila
¾ oz. orange liqueur
½ oz. lime juice

Shake with ice and strain into a glass.

MESA FRESCA

1½ oz. Dos Manos 100 percent blanco tequila
fresh grapefruit juice
1 oz. fresh lime juice

Pour into a highball glass over ice.

MEXICALI ROSE

1 oz. Buen Amigo tequila
4 oz. cranberry juice cocktail
½ oz. lime juice
lime slice for garnish

MEXICAN BANANA

1½ oz. Buen Amigo tequila
¾ oz. crème de banana

Pour ingredients into an old-fashioned glass with ice.

MEXICAN BANSHEE

1½ oz. tequila
¾ oz. crème de banana
3 oz. cream or half-and-half

Blend all ingredients with crushed ice and strain into a large cocktail glass.

MEXICAN COFFEE

¾ oz. Two Fingers tequila
¾ oz. Kahlua
3 oz. coffee

Fill with hot coffee in heated coffee mug.

MEXICAN COOLER

1½ oz. tequila
4 oz. red wine
½ oz. grenadine
½ oz. lemon juice
7UP
red cherry for garnish
lemon wedge for garnish

Pour first four ingredients into a tall glass over ice and top with a squirt of 7UP. Garnish with a red cherry and a lemon wedge.

MEXICAN COSMO

1 oz. Agavero tequila
1 oz. vodka
splash cranberry juice
splash lime juice

In a shaker, combine all ingredients with ice. Shake until cold. Pour into a martini glass. Garnish with a lime slice. Another Cosmo but with Agavero tequila.

MEXICAN DEW

1 oz. tequila
Mountain Dew

Pour the shot of tequila into a glass over ice and fill with Mountain Dew.

MEXICAN FIREWATER

6 oz. Corona
1 oz. Campbell's tomato juice
1 oz. Absolut Peppar
¼ oz. Tabasco Chipotle Pepper Sauce
dash Worcestershire sauce
1¾ oz. 1800 tequila
¼ oz. Tabasco Habanero Sauce
salt
2 lime wedges

Pour Corona into a partially salted pint glass. In a shaker, combine the tomato juice, Absolut Peppar, Tabasco Chipotle Pepper Sauce, and Worcestershire sauce. Shake with ice and strain into the pint glass. In a 2 oz. shot glass (small enough to drop into the pint glass), combine the tequila and Tabasco Habanero Sauce. Squeeze 1 lime wedge into the shot glass. Lick the salt from the pint glass, drop the shot into the pint glass, shoot, and bite the other lime wedge.

MEXICAN FLAG

1 shot white tequila
1 shot grenadine
1 shot crème de menthe

Layer the shots in order of the colors of the Mexican flag.

MEXICAN GOLD

1½ oz. Buen Amigo tequila
¼ oz. Goldschläger
¾ oz. Galliano

Pour the first two ingredients into an old-fashioned glass over ice. Float Galliano.

MEXICAN HIGH DIVE

2 oz. tequila
1 raw oyster
drop Tabasco chipotle pepper sauce

Pour into a glass with ice.

MEXICAN HOT CHOCOLATE

4 oz. Reserva del Señor almendrado tequila
32 oz. milk
1 tablet (¾ oz.) Ibrra chocolate

Heat milk in saucepan on high until scalded. Remove from heat. Put chocolate tablet in blender and chop. Add tequila. Pour hot milk in blender and mix well. (Be careful blending hot ingredients.) Makes 4 drinks.

MEXICAN ICED TEA

1½ oz. tequila gold
3 oz. beer (Corona Extra)
lime slice for garnish

Pour tequila and beer into a lowball glass over ice. Stir gently. Garnish with a lime slice.

MEXICAN LITTLE MAN

1 oz. tequila
1 oz. gin
1 oz. amaretto
cranberry-apple juice

Mix on the rocks in a tumbler.

MEXICAN MELON BALL

1½ oz. Dos Manos reposado tequila
½ cup fresh-squeezed honey dew melon juice
½ cup fresh-squeezed orange juice
orange slice for garnish

Shake with ice and strain into a rocks glass over ice. Garnish with an orange slice.

MEXICAN MERMAID

1 oz. premium tequila, chilled
1 triangular chunk fresh pineapple, generously dusted with sparkling
  colored-sugar crystals
dry and fruity champagne, chilled, to fill
splash blue curaçao
long twist of lime peel, preferably spiral cut

*Attach sugar-coated pineapple chunk to the rim of a champagne flute
glass. Add tequila and fill with champagne. Then add the blue curaçao
and a spiral of lime peel. Serve immediately. Tell guests to drop the
pineapple chunk into the drink for an added splash of bubbles.*

MEXICAN ROSE

1½ oz. Buen Amigo tequila
1 oz. lime juice
½ oz. grenadine (or crème de cassis)

Pour into an old-fashioned glass over ice.

MEXICAN THANKSGIVING

¾ oz. tequila
¾ oz. Wild Turkey
1 tbsp. Tabasco

Mix in a shot glass and serve.

MEXICAN WITCH

1½ oz. tequila
¾ oz. Strega

Pour into an old-fashioned glass over ice.

MEXICANA

1½ oz. tequila
1 oz. lemon juice
splash pineapple juice
splash grenadine

Shake with ice and strain into a cocktail glass.

MEXICOLA

2 oz. tequila
juice of ½ lime
Coca-Cola

Pour tequila and lime juice over ice cubes in a Collins glass. Fill with Coca-Cola and stir.

MEXXXICAN BERRY

¾ oz. XXX tequila
¾ oz. Chambord
¼ oz. triple sec
raspberry for garnish

Shake with ice and strain into a sugar-frosted Pony glass. Top with a raspberry.

MEXXXICAN FLAG

1 oz. grenadine
1 oz. crème de menthe
1 oz. XXX tequila

Layer by pouring each ingredient into a highball glass using a spoon.

MEXXXICAN SURFER

1 oz. XXX tequila
1 oz. rum
pineapple juice to fill

Pour first two ingredients into an old-fashioned glass. Fill with pineapple juice and ice, then stir.

MEXXXICANA

1½ oz. XXX tequila
1 oz. lemon juice
1 tbsp. pineapple juice
1 tsp. grenadine

Shake with ice and strain into cocktail glass.

MIDNITE MADNESS

2 oz. Oro Azul tequila
splash blackberry liqueur
splash mango puree
splash orange juice
ginger ale to top

Pour first four ingredients into a shaker and top with ginger ale. Shake and strain into martini glass.

MIRAGE

1½ oz. Buen Amigo tequila
1½ oz. orange juice
1½ oz. tonic water
lime wedge for garnish

Stir. Garnish with a lime wedge.

THE MISSIK

1 oz. tequila
1 oz. margarita mix
1 oz. cranberry-grape juice
1 oz. Mountain Dew

Mix in a cocktail glass.

MOCKINGBIRD

1¼ oz. Pepe Lopez gold tequila
2 tsp white crème de menthe
1 oz. fresh lime juice

Shake vigorously and strain into a chilled martini glass.

MOJITA DE CASA

1½ oz. Zapopan gold tequila
2 fresh sprigs of mint leaves
¾ oz. fresh lime juice
1 oz. simple syrup
mint sprig for garnish

Muddle mint leaves with simple syrup and lime juice in a mixing glass. Pour in Zapopan gold tequila and shake over cracked ice. Strain into a highball glass over ice. Add a splash of soda and garnish with a sprig of mint.

MONSTER ON THE BEACH

1½ oz. Buen Amigo tequila
2 oz. cranberry juice
splash lime juice
splash grenadine

Serve over ice.

MONTANA FIRE

1 oz. tequila
1 oz. peppermint schnapps
1 oz. cinnamon schnapps
½ oz. Tabasco

Stir well.

MONTEZUMA

1½ oz. tequila
1 oz. Madeira

Blend ingredients with ½ cup crushed ice in an electric blender at a low speed for a short length of time. Pour in champagne flute and serve.

MOOEY AGAVE

¾ oz. El Mayor reposado tequila
¾ oz. Kahlua
¾ oz. Amarula cream liqueur
¾ oz. Arrow amaretto
chocolate syrup to rim glass

Dip chilled martini glass into chocolate syrup. Shake well with ice and strain into the chocolate-rimmed, chilled martini glass.

MOONLIGHT MARGARITA

1½ oz. Buen Amigo tequila
1 oz. blue curaçao
1 oz. fresh lime juice
½ oz. lemon juice
lime slice for garnish

Squeeze fresh lime. Rub rim of cocktail glass with lime rind, dip into salt. Blend and pour into salt-rimmed glass. Garnish with a lime slice.

MOONRAKER

2 oz. XXX tequila
4 oz. pineapple juice
1½ oz. blue curaçao

Pour first two ingredients into a rocks glass over ice. Stir well. Drop the curaçao into the center of the drink.

MOONRAKER #2

1½ oz. tequila
4 oz. pineapple juice
½ oz. blue curaçao

Serve in a tall glass.

MORNING

1 oz. Buen Amigo tequila
1 oz. pineapple juice
1 oz. orange juice
splash triple sec
grenadine to top
lime slice for garnish

Pour first four ingredients into a glass and float grenadine on top. Garnish with a lime slice.

MORNING BREEZE

1½ oz. Don Julio reposado tequila
2 oz. ginger ale
2 oz. club soda
lime wedge for garnish

Pour into a chilled highball glass over ice. Garnish with a lime wedge.

MOUNTAIN MELTER

1½ oz. Jose Cuervo Especial tequila
3 oz. hot chocolate
splash triple sec
dollop whipped cream
½ tsp. cinnamon

In a cup with hot chocolate, add Jose Cuervo Especial and triple sec. Top with whipped cream and cinnamon.

MUPPET

½ part XXX tequila
½ part 7UP

Pour into a shot glass. Hit table, holding glass, so it doesn't spill. Drink.

MUT HUT

1 oz. tequila
½ oz. Kahlua
½ oz. Godiva
½ oz. Baileys

Serve in a shot glass.

NATURAL VANILLA MARGARITA

1 part Navan vanilla liqueur
2 parts silver tequila
1 part fresh lime juice

Shake with ice. Strain into a chilled martini glass.

NEED FOR SPEED

2 oz. tequila
3 oz. Sprite

Pour into a tall glass over ice.

NEON TEQUILA MONSTER

1 oz. Buen Amigo tequila
1 oz. Burnett's vodka
3 oz. orange juice

Serve in a tall glass with ice.

NEVER A SEVEN

1 oz. tequila
2 oz. rum
1 oz. Jack Daniel's
1 oz. Goldschlager
½ oz. Tabasco

Mix.

NEW LIFE

1½ oz. Buen Amigo tequila
1 lump sugar
3 dashes Angostura bitters
lemon twist for garnish

Muddle sugar and bitters in an old-fashioned glass and fill with crushed ice. Add Buen Amigo tequila. Garnish with a lemon twist.

NICK AT NIGHT

1½ oz. Cuervo gold tequila
1½ oz. peach schnapps
2 oz. sweet and sour mix
2 oz. cranberry juice

Shake with ice and pour into a Collins glass.

NIGHT & DAY

½ part XXX tequila
½ part coffee liqueur
½ part Coca-Cola

Serve in a shot glass.

NOBLE SUNSET

1 oz. Casa Noble crystal tequila
1 oz. amaretto
1 oz. orange juice
¼ oz. grenadine

Pour first three ingredients into an iced mixing glass. Shake and strain into a chilled cocktail glass. Slowly pour grenadine into layer.

NUCLEAR SUNRISE

1 oz. tequila
1 oz. beer
1 oz. orange juice
1 oz. grenadine
Jack Daniels whisky

Serve in a tall glass.

NYMPHOMANIAC

1 oz. XXX tequila
¼ oz. peach schnapps
¼ oz. Malibu rum

Shake and strain into a rocks glass.

OLD-FASHIONED

2 oz. XXX tequila
1 tsp. sugar
5 dashes bitters
sparkling water
maraschino cherries

Combine sugar, water and bitters in the bottom of a chilled old-fashioned glass. Fill with ice and add XXX tequila. Stir well. Drop in a cherry or two.

OLD GREEN AND GOLD

1 oz. tequila
1 oz. Galliano
dash blue curaçao
dash Goldschläger

Serve in a shot glass.

OLD LAY

1¼ oz. XXX tequila
¾ oz. triple sec
splash lime juice
dash grenadine

Shake first three ingredients with ice and strain into a chilled cocktail glass. Top with a dash of grenadine.

ONEHOUSE

1 part tequila
1 part Malibu coconut rum

Mix, then add ice.

ORANGE ED

1 oz. tequila
1 oz. triple sec
½ oz. Bacardi Limon
½ oz. Baileys Irish cream
½ oz. Jack Daniel's whisky
½ oz. vodka
½ oz. Absolut Mandarin
½ oz. Southern Comfort
½ oz. Kahlua
4 oz. orange juice

Blend and pour over ice in a highball glass. Makes two cocktails.

ORANGE HAZE

1½ shot tequila
1 shot De Kuyper triple sec
1 shot vodka
orange juice to fill
orange slice for garnish

Shake the first three ingredients and pour into a highball glass over ice. Top with orange juice. Garnish with an orange slice.

OXBEND

1½ oz. Jose Cuervo tequila
½ oz. Southern Comfort
4 oz. orange juice
dash grenadine

Fill glass with ice, add all ingredients, and stir.

PABLITO

Equal parts:
XXX tequila
Cointreau
orange juice

Shake with ice and pour into a martini glass.

PACIFIC BREEZE

1½ oz. Oro Azul anejo tequila
juice of 1 lime
2 oz. passion fruit
lime wedge for garnish

Shake well with ice and pour into a Collins glass. Garnish with a lime wedge.

PACIFIC SUNSHINE

1½ oz. tequila
1½ oz. blue curaçao
1½ oz. sour mix
dash bitters
salt to rim glass
lemon wheel for garnish

Shake with ice and strain into a chilled parfait glass with a salted rim. Garnish with a lemon wheel.

PALOMA

2 oz. Casa Noble reposado tequila
½ oz. lime juice
fresh grapefruit juice to fill
splash tonic water

Pour first two ingredients into a cocktail glass and fill with grapefruit juice. Top with a splash of tonic water.

PANTHER

1½ oz. Jose Cuervo tequila
½ oz. sweet and sour mix

Pour into an old fashioned glass over several ice cubes. Stir well and serve. Keep ready for the Pink Panther.

PARALYZER

1½ oz. tequila
¾ oz. white crème de cacao
¾ oz. Kahlua
cream to fill

Shake first three ingredients with ice and strain into a lowball glass. Fill with cream.

PARKEROO

1 oz. tequila
3 oz. dry sherry
lemon twist for garnish

Pour into champagne flute and garnish with a lemon twist.

PASSION POTION

1 oz. agavero tequila
1 oz. 1800 anejo tequila
1 maraschino cherry

Serve in a shot glass over ice.

PASSIONATE RITA

1½ oz. tequila
1 oz. passion fruit liqueur
½ oz. lime juice

Shake, don't stir.

PATRON CITRUS CRUSH

1½ oz. Patron reposado tequila
½ oz. Patron citronge tequila
5 kumquats
¾ oz. rock candy syrup
sugarcane stick for garnish

Cut kumquats in halves and place them in a shaker tin. Add syrup and muddle for five to ten seconds. Add ice, Patron reposado tequila and Patron citronge tequila. Shake and pour (do not strain) into a double old-fashioned glass. Garnish with a sugarcane stick.

PATRON PERFECT COSMO

2 oz. Patron silver tequila
¾ oz. Patron citronge
splash cranberry juice
lime squeeze
lime wheel for garnish

Shake well with ice and strain into a martini glass. Garnish with a lime wheel.

PEACH MARGARITA

1½ oz. tequila
1 oz. peach schnapps
1 tsp. Cointreau
1 oz. lime juice or juice of half a lime
lime wedge for garnish

Shake well with ice and strain into a salt-rimmed cocktail glass. Garnish with a lime wedge.

PEPE COLA

2 oz. Pepe Lopez tequila
½ oz. lime juice
½ can cola

Mix Pepe Lopez tequila and lime juice in a tall glass with ice. Fill with cola and stir.

PEPE KAZI

1½ oz. Pepe Lopez tequila
2 oz. cranberry juice
½ oz. triple sec
1 tsp. lime juice

Shake with ice and strain into a glass.

PEPE PUNCH

1 liter chilled Pepe Lopez tequila
1 750 ml. bottle chilled champagne
2 750 ml. bottles chilled sauterne
64 oz. fresh fruit (cubes or balls)

Put all ingredients in a large punch bowl. Add ice cubes just before serving.

PENETRATOR IV

½ oz. tequila
½ oz. Kahlua
½ oz. Baileys Irish cream
½ oz. Tia Maria
½ oz. vodka
½ oz. Malibu rum
½ oz. Galliano
⅙ oz. milk

Pour the first seven ingredients over two ice cubes and add the milk. Stir.

PEPPERITA

1¼ oz. gold tequila
⅔ oz. Grand Marnier
juice of ½ lime
1 tsp. Tabasco green pepper sauce
salt to rim glass
lime slice for garnish

Rub the rim of a goblet with the cut side of a lime, then dip rim into a saucer of salt. Fill glass with ice. Pour first three ingredients into an ice-filled cocktail shaker or pitcher, and shake or stir vigorously. Strain into ice-filled glass. Shake in Tabasco green pepper sauce and stir. Garnish with a slice of lime.

PETROLEUM

1 shot Jose Cuervo tequila
dash Tabasco
dash Maggi seasoning

Serve as a shot. It looks like used motor oil, and tastes even worse.

PETTING ZOO

½ oz. tequila
½ oz. rum
½ oz. Wild Turkey
1 oz. White Horse scotch
4 oz. Gatorade

Blend with ice until ice is crushed.

PHAT CAT MARGARITA

1¼ oz. Tarantula azul tequila
½ oz. triple sec
½ oz. blue curaçao
1 oz. pineapple juice
2 oz. sweet and sour
lime wedge for garnish

Shake vigorously with ice and pour into a 14-oz. Collins glass. Garnish with a lime wedge.

PICK ME UP JOSE

½ oz. Jose Cuervo tequila
½ oz. Bacardi 151

Serve in a shot glass.

PICOSA

1⅓ oz. tequila
⅔ oz. Cointreau
3 oz. orange juice
2 dashes Tabasco

Shake well with ice and pour into a glass.

PIMP DADDY

2 oz. tequila
1 oz. vodka
1 oz. lemon juice
cranberry juice to fill

Pour into a beer mug with ice and garnish with a lemon slice.

PINA

1½ oz. Jose Cuervo tequila
3 oz. pineapple juice
1 oz. lime juice
1 tsp. sugar syrup

Add all ingredients to a mixing glass with ice. Shake and strain into glass with ice.

PINATA

1½ oz. Buen Amigo tequila
5 oz. pineapple juice
¼ oz. club soda
fresh pineapple for garnish

Serve in a tall glass. Top with club soda. Garnish with fresh pineapple.

PINEAPPLE SUNRISE

1½ oz. white tequila
3 oz. pineapple juice
1 oz. lime juice
1 tsp. powdered sugar

Shake with ice and strain into a cocktail glass.

PINK CAD

1½ oz. Jose Cuervo tequila
1 oz. lime juice
½ oz. triple sec
½ oz. Grand Marnier
4 oz. sweet and sour mix

Pour over ice and stir.

PINK CAD WITH HAWAIIAN PLATES

1¼ oz. Don Alvaro tequila
2 oz. pineapple juice
2 oz. cranberry juice
½ oz. sweet and sour mix
lime wedge for garnish

Serve in a rocks glass. Garnish with a lime wedge.

PINK DIAMOND

1½ oz. Tequila Rose
3 oz. champagne

Mix very slowly and pour into a champagne glass.

PINK PONY

2 oz. XXX tequila
⅓ cup chilled cranberry juice
¼ cup chilled apple juice
chilled club soda or seltzer water

Pour first three ingredients into a rocks glass over ice. Top with club soda.

PINK PANTHER

1½ oz. Buen Amigo tequila
½ oz. grenadine
2 oz. cream or half-and-half

Blend with ice and strain. Pour into chilled cocktail glass.

PINK RUSSIAN

1½ oz. Tequila Rose
1 oz. Polar Ice vodka
¾ oz. white crème de cacao
1 oz. half-and-half

Mix and serve on the rocks.

PINK SPIDER

1¼ oz. Tarantula azul tequila
1 oz. pineapple juice
1 oz. pink grapefruit juice
½ oz. grenadine
lime squeezes
lime slice for garnish

Shake vigorously with ice and strain into glass with ice. Garnish with a lime slice.

PIPER

2 oz. Jose Cuervo tequila
½ oz. lemon juice
crushed ice
4 oz. black coffee
½ oz. brown crème de cacao

PISSED OFF JAPANESE MINNOW FARMER

¼ oz. tequila silver
¼ oz. vodka
¼ oz. gin
¼ oz. rum
¼ oz. Chambord raspberry liqueur
¼ oz. Midori
½ oz. sweet and sour mix

Shake vigorously with ice and strain into a highball glass over ice cubes.

PLASSE KNOCK OUT

1½ oz. tequila
1½ oz. vodka
2½ oz. peach schnapps
orange juice to fill

Mix first three ingredients in a highball glass and fill with orange juice.

PLAYER

2½ shots XXX tequila
½ glass orange juice
½ glass strawberry daiquiri

Pour ingredients into a frozen beer mug. Wait two minutes to serve cold.

POLLA

2 oz. tequila
1 oz. lemon juice
Squirt to fill
salt to taste

Gently mix first two ingredients in a tall glass. Fill with Squirt and add salt to taste.

POLLENADE

½ oz. tequila
½ oz. Drambuie
½ oz. Chambord raspberry liqueur
2 oz. lemonade

Combine the first three ingredients and shake. Serve over ice in a Collins glass. Float lemonade to top.

POMEGRANATE MARGARITA

1½ oz. Gran Centenario reposado tequila
½ oz. Cointreau
¾ oz. Grand Marnier
½ oz. Pom Wonderful pomegranate juice or a couple dozen seeds
¾ oz. fresh squeezed lime juice (half a lime)
½ oz. fresh grapefruit juice
thin lime wedge for garnish

Shake well with ice and strain into a chilled martini glass. Garnish with a thin lime wedge.

POMEGRANATE PERFECTION

1½ oz. Oro Azul anejo tequila
½ oz. apple brandy
2 oz. pomegranate juice
2 oz. fresh lemon juice
dash cinnamon
cinnamon stick for garnish

Shake well with ice and strain into a 12-oz. glass over ice. Garnish with a cinnamon stick.

PRAIRIE FIRE

1 oz. tequila
as much Tabasco as you can handle

Serve as a shot. Not for those with a weak stomach! Try it with all five Tabasco sauces—not all at once!

PRAYING MANTIS

1½ oz. Jose Cuervo tequila
1 tsp. lemon juice
2 tsp. lime juice
4 oz. Coca-Cola

Shake first three ingredients. Pour into a tall glass over ice. Fill with cola.

PRICKLY AGAVE

1½ oz. Patron silver tequila
½ oz. Patron citronge
1 oz. prickly pear puree
1½ oz. fresh sweet and sour
Malibu mango to float
lemon wheel for garnish

Shake with ice and serve straight up or on the rocks. Garnish with a lemon wheel.

PRICKLY CACTUS

2 shots Reserva del Señor almendrado tequila
Baileys Irish cream

Pour tequila into an 8 oz. tumbler glass half-filled with ice. Fill with Baileys Irish cream.

PUKE

½ oz. tequila
½ oz. Everclear
½ oz. Jack Daniel's whisky
½ oz. Jim Beam bourbon whisky
½ oz. Yukon Jack
½ oz. vodka

Shake with ice and pour into a highball glass.

PULCO

2 oz. Jose Cuervo 1800 tequila
1½ oz. lime juice
splash orange juice
½ oz. Cointreau

Serve on the rocks. Do not shake.

PURPLE GECKO

1½ oz. tequila
½ oz. blue curaçao
½ oz. red curaçao
1 oz. cranberry juice
1 oz. sour mix
½ oz. lime juice
lime wedge for garnish

Shake with ice and pour into a salt-rimmed cocktail glass. Garnish with a lime wedge.

PURPLE HAZE

½ oz. Jose Cuervo tequila
½ oz. vodka
½ oz. rum
1 oz. sour mix
½ oz. Chambord
½ oz. gin
lime wedge for garnish

Shake with ice and pour into a salt-rimmed glass. Garnish with a lime wedge.

PURPLE PANCHO

1 oz. tequila
½ oz. blue curaçao
½ oz. sloe gin
2 oz. lime juice
2 oz. sour mix
lime wedge for garnish

Shake with ice and pour into a salt-rimmed cocktail glass. Garnish with a lime wedge.

QUAALUDE

Equal parts:
XXX tequila
Baileys Irish cream
Grand Mariner

Stir over ice. Serve as a shot or on the rocks.

QUICK SILVER

1 part Jose Cuervo tequila
1 part triple sec
1 part anisette

Serve in a lowball glass.

RABID DOG

3 oz. Tequila Rose
12 dashes Tabasco Green Pepper Sauce
1 cup ice
jalapeño pepper for garnish

Blend until creamy. Pour into 6 oz. margarita glass. Garnish with jalapeño pepper.

RAINBOW

1½ oz. tequila
½ oz. grenadine
1 oz. lemon juice
1 oz. pineapple juice
1 oz. orange juice
Squirt or ginger ale to top

Pour first five ingredients into a tall glass with ice. Top with Squirt or ginger ale.

RAMSEY

1 shot Jose Cuervo tequila
1 shot milk
1 shot Irish cream
1 shot coffee liqueur

Mix in a tall glass, heavy on the ice.

RASPBERRY MARGARITA

1½ oz. Buen Amigo tequila
1 oz. triple sec
1 oz. lime juice
½ cup frozen raspberries
fresh raspberries for garnish

Blend. Garnish with fresh raspberries.

RATTLER

1½ oz. Jose Cuervo tequila
2 oz. grapefruit juice
¼ oz. lime juice
splash triple sec

Serve on the rocks.

RATTLESNAKE

3 parts XXX tequila
2 parts amaretto
1 part Kahlua
cream to top

*Layer first three ingredients in a pony or shot glass and top with cream.
Or, shake first three ingredients and strain into a glass. Top with cream.*

REARBUSTER

1 oz. Jose Cuervo Especial gold tequila
1 oz. Kahlua coffee liqueur
cranberry juice to fill
lemon wedge for garnish

Pour first two ingredients into a highball glass with ice. Fill with cranberry juice. Garnish with a lemon wedge and an umbrella, stir, and serve with a straw.

RED BEARD

2 oz. tequila
½ oz. sloe gin
2 oz. cranberry juice

Stir in a highball glass.

RED CACTUS

1½ oz. Buen Amigo tequila
4 oz. Oregon raspberry puree
1½ oz. Sunkist sweet and sour mix
½ cup ice
lime wheel for garnish

Blend. Garnish with a lime wheel.

RED FACE

1½ oz. Jose Cuervo tequila
1 tsp. cranberry liqueur
4 oz. cranberry juice
lime wedge

Serve in a tall glass.

RED HOOKER

2 parts tequila
lemon juice to taste
1 part grenadine

*Pour the first two ingredients into a shot glass. Add grenadine carefully.
A great sweet and sour shot.*

RED HOT CHILI PEPPER

1 oz. gold tequila
4 drops Tabasco
ginger beer to fill

Pour first two ingredients into a highball glass and fill with ginger beer.

RED HOT MAMA

½ oz. tequila
½ oz. orange juice
½ oz. tomato juice

*Stir with ice and strain into a shot glass for a shooter or into an old-
fashioned glass with ice for a cocktail.*

RED MONSTER

⅓ Buen Amigo tequila
⅓ orange juice
⅓ tomato juice

Serve in a shot glass.

REST IN PEACE

1 oz. Jose Cuervo tequila
1 oz. vodka
1 oz. Jack Daniel's
1 oz. Jim Beam

Serve over ice. Drink slowly.

ROADKILL

1 oz. Jose Cuervo tequila
1 oz. whisky
1 oz. Hot Damn cinnamon schnapps

Shake. Serve in a shot glass.

ROCKET FUEL

1 part Jose Cuervo tequila
2 parts vodka
1 part rum
1 part triple sec
1 part gin

Shake. Serve in a tall glass with crushed ice.

ROOSTER TAIL

1 shot Jose Cuervo tequila
1 shot tomato juice
1 shot orange juice
dash salt
2 splashes Tabasco sweet & spicy pepper sauce

Shake.

ROSE BUD

1½ oz. Tequila Rose
½ oz. coconut rum

Serve in a shot glass.

THE ROSE DANCER

1 oz. Tequila Rose
1 oz. silver rum
½ oz. triple sec
fresh diced peaches
club soda to top
whipped cream to top
strawberry for garnish

Pour first three ingredients into a glass; top with club soda and whipped cream. Mix and serve with a strawberry on top.

ROSE PARFAIT

2 oz. Tequila Rose
1 oz. banana liqueur
2 oz. milk or heavy cream
whipped cream to top
graham cracker crumbs for sprinkling
strawberry for garnish

Blend well. Pour into a hurricane glass. Top with whipped cream and sprinkle with graham cracker crumbs. Garnish with one strawberry.

ROSITA

1½ oz. tequila
1 oz. Campari
½ oz. dry vermouth
½ oz. sweet vermouth

Pour over crushed ice and stir well.

ROSY NIPPLE

1 oz. Tequila Rose
1 oz. butterscotch schnapps

Mix.

THE ROXY

1½ oz. El Tesoro silver tequila
1½ oz. honey syrup (1 oz. honey + ½ oz. hot water)
4 strawberries
4 cilantro sprigs
3 oz. pasteurized or fresh egg white
10 shakes Tabasco

In a whipped cream canister add ¾ oz. honey syrup, 3 oz. egg white, and Tabasco sauce. Put top on and keep cold. When ready, add CO_2 cartridge and shake well. In a mixing glass add rest of honey, 3 strawberries, and cilantro, and muddle well. Add tequila and ice, and shake well. Strain through a mesh strainer (double strain) over ice in a tall glass. Put tip of whipped cream canister into drink and fill with foam. Garnish with 4th strawberry, with a cilantro sprig stuck into its top.

RUDE COSMOPOLITAN

1 oz. Jose Cuervo Clásico tequila
½ oz. orange liqueur
1 oz. cranberry juice
splash lime juice
lime wedge for garnish

Shake with ice and pour into a glass. Garnish with a lime wedge.

RUSTY NAVEL

1 part tequila
1 part amaretto
1 part peach schnapps

Stir. Serve on the rocks.

SALSA MARGARITA

1 part tequila
1 cup ice
3 parts margarita mix
2 dashes Tabasco chipotle pepper sauce
cilantro sprig for garnish
lime slice for garnish

Blend. Garnish with a sprig of fresh cilantro and a lime slice. Salted rim optional.

SAN DIEGO STYLE

6 oz. tequila 100 percent agave
6 oz. Sprite
2 oz. Cointreau
6 oz. can frozen limeade

Blend with ice (except Sprite). Pour, top with Sprite, and drink. Serves 3.

SAN DIEGO SUNRISE

4 oz. tequila
8 oz. orange juice
2 oz. amaretto
1 tbsp. vanilla
1 cup pineapple and papaya ice cream

Blend two cups of crushed ice with the first four ingredients until slushy. Then add the ice cream and blend on medium until slushy.

SANG DE DRAGON

¾ oz. gold tequila (or white)
¾ oz. Jack Daniel's whisky
4 drops Tabasco

Mix the first two ingredients in a shot glass. Put in Tabasco.

SANGRITA

3 oz. tequila
16 oz. tomato juice
8 oz. orange juice
2 oz. lime juice
2 tsp. hot sauce
2 tsp. minced onion
2 tsp. Worcestershire sauce

SANGRITA CHASER

3 oz. tequila
8 oz. freshly squeezed orange juice
2–4 oz. fresh lime juice
1 tbsp. grenadine syrup
1 tbsp. salt
¼ tbsp. chile piquín, or to taste

Blend. Serve in a large punch bowl.

SANTA FE MAGGIE

1¼ oz. Buen Amigo tequila
½ oz. triple sec
2 oz. sweet and sour mix
2 oz. cranberry juice
lime wedge for garnish

Garnish with lime wedge dropped into glass.

SANTA MARIA

1 oz. gold tequila
1 oz. Captain Morgan's spiced rum
dash sweet vermouth
orange slice for garnish

Shake gently with ice and strain into a chilled cocktail glass. Garnish with an orange slice.

SAUVE

1½ oz. gold tequila
dash Pernod licorice liqueur
1 oz. pineapple juice
1 oz. Sunny Delight orange juice
1 tbsp. orgeat syrup

Shake ingredients in a cocktail shaker with ice. Strain into glass.

SCHWAB A WABBA

½ oz. tequila
½ oz. blue curaçao
½ oz. vodka
½ oz. peach schnapps
4 oz. lemonade
3 oz. orange juice
3 oz. white rum, or to taste (optional)

Mix well.

SCORPION'S STING

½ oz. tequila
½ oz. rum
splash of Tabasco chipotle pepper sauce

Serve in a shot glass.

SCRATCH AND SNIFF

1½ oz. Jose Cuervo tequila
2 oz. orange juice
2 oz. pineapple juice
½ oz. Chambord

Shake. Serve in a tall glass with ice.

SCREAMER

¼ oz. Jose Cuervo tequila
¼ oz. vodka
¼ oz. rum
¼ oz. triple sec
¼ oz. gin

Shake and strain into a shot glass. Shoot.

SCUBA JUICE

2 oz. tequila
1 oz. orange juice
1 oz. lemon juice
1 oz. cranberry juice
1 oz. grapefruit juice
lemon twist for garnish
lime wheel for garnish
orange wheel for garnish
cherry for garnish

Shake and serve in a tall glass with two straws. Garnish with a lemon twist, a lime wheel, an orange wheel, and a cherry.

SEEGER'S MORMON KILLER

2 oz. Jamaica rum
1 oz. mezcal
1 oz. whisky (151 Proof)
2 oz. Dr. Pepper

Pour into a Collins glass.

SEXXX IN RIO

2 oz. XXX tequila
1 tangerine, peeled and cut into wedges
2 tsp. caster sugar
juice of ½ lime

Place the sugar in an old-fashioned glass or tumbler and add the lime. With a muddler or the back of a spoon, break down the tangerine so that its juice is absorbed by the sugar. Add the crushed ice, and then stir in XXX tequila and lime juice.

SEXXX ON THE BEACH

1 oz. XXX tequila
¾ oz. each: Chambord & peach schnapps
splashes of pineapple, orange, and cranberry juices

Shake with ice and serve in a Collins glass or decorative glass.

SEXXXY BEAST

1 oz. XXX tequila
1 oz. Goldschlager
1 oz. Jagermeister

Pour XXX tequila into a glass, then Jagermeister. Top with Goldschlager.

SEXY LEMONADE

½ oz. 1800 reposado tequila
1 oz. triple sec
½ oz. 7UP
sweet and sour mix to fill
lemon slice

Pour first three ingredients into an ice-filled highball glass. Fill with sweet and sour and add sugar. Drop in a slice of lemon and stir well.

SHADY LADY

1 oz. XXX tequila
1 oz. melon liqueur
4 oz. grapefruit juice
lime slice for garnish

Pour into a highball glass over ice and stir. Garnish with a slice of lime.

SHAG PILE

2 oz. tequila
1 oz. rum
1 oz. vodka
beer

Shake 2 oz. tequila with ice. Add vodka and rum, shake. Add this to a glass of beer. Then pour in the remaining tequila over the back of a spoon.

SHAKER

1½ oz. tequila
3 oz. pineapple juice
½ oz. lemon juice or lemonade
½ tsp. grenadine

Shake well with ice and strain into a cocktail glass.

SHANDY

1¼ oz. Buen Amigo tequila
splash Tabasco Garlic Sauce
7 oz. draft beer

Serve in a chilled mug.

SHARK

1½ oz. tequila
1 oz. vodka
dash Tabasco

Serve in a shot glass.

SHARK ATTACK

1½ oz. tequila
½ oz. sloe gin
½ oz. Cointreau
sugar to rim glass

Shake and strain. Serve as a shot with sugared rim.

SIDE OUT

1½ oz. Buen Amigo tequila
1 oz. triple sec
2 oz. cranberry juice
1½ oz. lime juice.

Blend with ice.

SIESTA

1½ oz. Buen Amigo tequila
¾ oz. lime juice
½ oz. sloe gin

Blend or shake with ice and strain. Pour into a chilled cocktail glass.

SILK PANTY RAID

1 oz. each:
XXX tequila
peach schnapps
cranberry juice

Stir with ice and serve in a chilled cocktail glass.

SILK STOCKINGS

1½ oz. XXX tequila
1 oz. crème de cacao
1½ oz. cream
dash grenadine
cinnamon for sprinkling

Shake with crushed ice. Strain into a cocktail glass and sprinkle cinnamon on top.

SILVER BLAZE

1 oz. Sauza tequila (blanco)
½ oz. Beefeater dry gin
½ oz. white crème de menthe
½ oz. apricot brandy
2 oz. light cream
drop grenadine
lemon juice
mint sprig for garnish

Shake over ice then strain into a well-chilled martini glass. Garnish with a sprig of mint.

SILVER DEVIL

1 oz. tequila
1 oz. peppermint schnapps

Layer in a shot glass.

SIXTY-9

1 oz. reposado tequila
½ oz. peach vodka
splash cranberry juice
splash pineapple juice
splash sour mix
orange slice for garnish

Shake over ice and serve in a rocks glass straight up. Garnish with an orange slice.

SLEEPER

1 oz. tequila
1 oz. Galliano
1 oz. Kahlua
cola

Shake with ice and strain into a highball glass with crushed ice. Top with cola.

SLOE TEQUILA

1 oz. tequila
½ oz. sloe gin
1 tbsp. lime juice
cucumber peel for garnish

Blend with ½ cup of ice at low speed and pour into an old-fashioned glass. Garnish with a twist of cucumber peel.

SLOW AND STEADY

1 oz. tequila
1 pint of beer
pinch salt (plus more to rim glass)
juice of ½ lemon

Add tequila, salt, and lemon juice to the beer and shake well. Rim the mug with salt and serve.

SLOW BUZZ

1 part tequila
1 part passion fruit liqueur or Chambord
1 part peach schnapps

Mix and add ice. Add club soda if you want a slower buzz.

SLOW COMFORTABLE SCREW UP AGAINST THE WALL MEXICAN STYLE

½ oz. Sauza tequila
½ oz. sloe gin
½ oz. Southern Comfort
½ oz. Galliano
orange juice to fill

Build in a highball glass and fill with orange juice.

SMOKEY CINNAMON APPLE MARGARITA

1 oz. tequila
2 oz. apple juice
½ oz. cinnamon schnapps
Tabasco chipotle pepper sauce

Shake well with ice and pour into a chilled cocktail glass.

SMOKEY MARGARITA

2 oz. tequila
1 oz. triple sec
1 oz. fresh lime juice
¾ tsp. simple syrup
½ oz. mezcal

Shake first four ingredients and pour into a rocks glass over ice. Float mezcal to top.

SMOOTH CASA NOBLE

2 oz. Casa Noble reposado tequila

Put two ice cubes in an old fashioned glass and add the tequila slowly. Turn gently for five to ten seconds and serve.

SNAKE BITE

1 part tequila
1 part Jack Daniel's whisky

An excellent drink, but like the name, it has a bite!

SNAKE IN THE GRASS

2 oz. tequila
40 oz. King Kobra or a malt beverage
2 tbsp. sugar
2 tbsp. honey

Drink half of the 40 oz. then pour the remaining ingredients into the bottle. Shake with ice and drink quickly.

SOUTH OF THE BORDER

1 oz. tequila
¾ oz. coffee brandy
½ oz. vodka
juice of ½ lime
lime slice for garnish

Shake with ice and strain into a sour glass. Garnish with a lime slice.

SOUTH OF THE BORDER #2

4 oz. Tabasco Bloody Mary Mix, original or extra spicy
1½ oz. tequila
¼ tsp. lime juice
bell pepper stick for garnish

Shake and pour into a salt-rimmed glass over ice. Garnish with a bell pepper stick.

SPANISH FLY

1 oz. tequila
1 oz. Cuarenta Y Tres
dash cinnamon for garnish

Build in a lowball glass. Garnish with cinnamon.

SPANISH MOSS

1 oz. tequila
1 oz. coffee liqueur
1 oz. crème de menthe

Stir with ice and strain into a glass.

SPARKLE

3 oz. tequila
½ bottle Jones soda (your favorite flavor)
2 oz. Sprite

Blend tequila with crushed ice. Pour into a tall glass and fill with soda and Sprite.

SPICE OF LIFE

1 oz. tequila
3 cherry tomatoes
5 mint leaves
½ oz. vanilla gomme
dash lime juice
3 drops Tabasco

Muddle cherry tomatoes with mint leaves, lime juice, and vanilla gomme. Add tequila and Tabasco. Shake well with ice and strain into a glass.

SPICED SANGRIA SUNRISE

2 oz. tequila
1½ oz. orange juice
2 tbsp. grenadine
4 oz. lime juice
2 oz. Tabasco chipotle pepper sauce
16 oz. wine, red
8 oz. simple syrup
pinch salt
1 cup crushed ice

Blend. Depending on the size of the blender, you may have to split ingredients in ½ and blend ½ at a time. Blend about 1 minute, pour into a pitcher and chill.

SPIDER BITE

1½ oz. Tarantula Azul tequila
energy drink (Red Bull)

Serve in a 14-oz. glass over ice.

SPIKE

1½ oz. Buen Amigo tequila
3 oz. ruby red grapefruit juice
dash bitters
orange wheel for garnish

Stir. Garnish with an orange wedge.

SSAB DREAM

2 oz. tequila
½ oz. apricot brandy
2 oz. cream
7UP

Shake first three ingredients with ice and strain into a cocktail glass. Fill with 7UP.

STINGER TEQUILA

2 parts XXX tequila
2 parts white crème de menthe

Shake well with ice and strain into a chilled martini glass.

STRAWBERRY BLOND

1 oz. Tequila Rose
½ oz. triple sec
½ oz. banana liqueur
¼ oz. spiced rum
1 oz. strawberry mix
orange slice, cherry, or strawberry for garnish

Add ice, blend until frozen. Garnish with an orange slice, cherry, or strawberry.

STRAWBERRY KISS

1 oz. Tequila Rose
½ oz. white rum
1 oz. chocolate liqueur
1 oz. half-and-half

Shake with ice and strain into a martini glass.

STRAWBERRY MARGARITA

1 oz. tequila
½ oz. Cointreau
½ oz. strawberry schnapps
1 oz. lemon or lime juice
1 oz. fresh or frozen strawberries
salt to rim glass

Shake well with ice and strain into a salt-rimmed glass.

STRAWBERRY S'MORE

1¼ oz. Tequila Rose
½ oz. McCormick vanilla vodka
¼ oz. butterscotch schnapps
hot chocolate to fill
jumbo marshmallows
chocolate syrup

Build first three ingredients in a glass or mug. Fill with hot chocolate.
Float two jumbo marshmallows. Drizzle chocolate syrup on top.

STRAWBERRY SPLIT

½ oz. Tequila Rose
½ oz. Tequila Rose strawberry liqueur
½ oz. coffee liqueur

Layer in a shot glass.

STRAWBERRY TRUFFLE

1 oz. Tequila Rose cocoa
1 oz. Tequila Rose strawberry liqueur
½ oz. half-and-half

Pour into a highball glass with ice in the order listed. Garnish with a
chocolate-dipped strawberry and serve.

SUBMARINE

1 shot XXX tequila
beer to fill

Fill a shot glass with XXX tequila. Very slowly put the shot upside down inside a beer mug, making sure the tequila stays inside the shot glass. Slowly fill the mug with beer. Try not to mix the tequila with the beer. Drink it all in one shot.

SUMMER'S STRAWBERRY ROSE

2 oz. Tequila Rose
1½ oz. Bacardi white rum
2 oz. strawberry mix

Blend with ice until consistency is smooth and creamy.

SUNBURN

1 oz. tequila
1 oz. Cointreau
cranberry juice to fill

Pour into a Collins glass with ice and enjoy.

SWASHBUCKLER

1¼ oz. Cuervo gold tequila
¾ oz. Grand Marnier
4 oz. sweet and sour mix
Hawaiian fruit punch

Pour the first three ingredients into a 16-oz. glass over ice. Top with Hawaiian fruit punch.

SWEET CASA NOBLE

1 oz. Casa Noble gold tequila
peach juice
splash grenadine
lime slice for garnish

Pour tequila into a Collins glass over ice and top with peach juice. Add the grenadine and garnish with a slice of lime.

SWEET CHARITY

1½ oz. Gran Centenario Plata tequila
¾ oz. fresh-squeezed grapefruit juice
¾ oz. fresh-squeezed orange juice
½ oz. crème de cassis
juice of ½ lemon wedge
frozen melon ball (honeydew or musk) for garnish

Prepare melon balls and freeze overnight. Shake all liquid ingredients well with ice and strain into a chilled martini glass. Garnish with frozen melon ball. Alternatively garnish with an orange peel flamed over the top.

SWEET ESTELLE

1 oz. tequila
1 oz. Kahlua
milk to fill

Pour first two ingredients into a glass over ice and fill with milk.

SWEET SEXXX

2 oz. XXX tequila
2 oz. crème de cacao
1 can evaporated milk
1 part grenadine
cinnamon for sprinkling

Blend first four ingredients with ice at medium speed until smooth. Pour into a chilled tumbler. Sprinkle cinnamon on top.

SWEET SOUTHERN TEA

1½ oz. tequila
1½ oz. vodka
1½ oz. gin
1½ oz. rum
1½ oz. triple sec
1½ oz. sour mix
splash amaretto

Shake with ice. Serve in a tall glass.

TBT

2 shots De Kuyper triple sec
1 shot De Kuyper crème de bananes
1 shot tequila

Layer the ingredients carefully in a shot glass using the order listed above.

T.K.O.

Equal parts:
XXX tequila
Kahlua
ouzo
lime juice to top

Shake tequila and cream. Strain into a glass over crushed ice. Top with layer of lime juice.

TLC

2 oz. Tarantula reposado tequila
½ oz. cream
½ oz. lime juice

Shake first two ingredients. Strain into a glass over crushed ice and top with a layer of lime juice.

TNP

2 shots tequila
1 shot Noilly Prat dry
large dash De Kuyper grenadine
cherry for garnish

Shake and serve in a cocktail glass. Garnish with a cherry.

TNT

1½ oz. Tarantula Plata tequila
4 oz. tonic water
splash lime juice
lime slice for garnish

*Pour first two ingredients into a 10 oz. footed highball glass over ½ cup
ice. Mix in lime juice and garnish with a lime slice.*

TVR

1 oz. tequila
1 oz. vodka
1 can Red Bull Energy Drink

Stir over ice in a tall glass.

TABASCO DIABLO

1 oz. gold tequila
½ oz. blue curaçao
2 oz. lime juice
Tabasco habanero pepper sauce to rim glass
rock salt to rim glass
lime wedge for garnish

*Blend with ice and serve in cocktail glass rimmed with Tabasco habanero
pepper sauce and rock salt. Garnish with a lime wedge.*

THE TALL COCKTAIL

2 oz. Tarantula reposado tequila
½ oz. lemonade
squirt of lime

Serve in a tall glass with ice.

TARANTULA BITE

1½ oz. Tarantula Azul tequila
½ oz. triple sec
½ oz. fresh lime juice
3 oz. sweet and sour
splash grenadine
lime wedge for garnish

Shake first four ingredients vigorously with ice and pour into a 14-oz. Collins glass. Top with a splash, about ⅛ oz., of grenadine and garnish with a lime wedge.

TARANTULA CACTUS COOLER

1½ oz. Tarantula Plata tequila
½ oz. peppermint schnapps
club soda
lime wheel for garnish

Pour Tarantula Plata and club soda into a tall glass over ice. Top with peppermint schnapps. Garnish with a lime wheel.

TARANTULA CARAMBA!

1½ oz. Tarantula reposado tequila
3 oz. grapefruit juice
1 tbsp. sugar
club soda to fill

Shake first three ingredients with well-cracked ice. Fill with club soda and serve in a highball glass.

TARANTULA CRANDADDY

1 oz. Tarantula Plata tequila
1 oz. triple sec
3 oz. cranberry juice

Stir in a large glass over ice.

TARANTULA SLAMMER

1½ oz. Tarantula reposado tequila
½ oz. St. Germain
2 oz. Sprite

TARANTULA STINGER

2 oz. Tarantula Plata tequila
¼ oz. crème de menthe (green liqueur)

Shake. Serve straight up or on the rocks.

TAROPOLITAN

1 oz. Tarantula reposado tequila
3 oz. cranberry juice
splash lime juice

Shake and pour into a chilled martini glass.

THE TEEF

2 oz. tequila (or to taste)
½ oz. St. Germain
squeeze lemon
Pepsi-Cola

Pour first three ingredients into a highball glass over ice and fill with Pepsi-Cola.

TEQ AND TEA

1½ oz. tequila
6 oz. iced tea (sweetened)

Mix over ice.

TEQUIL O'NEIL

1¼ oz. Tarantula reposado tequila
¼ oz. orange juice
⅛ oz. club soda

Serve in a shot glass and slam.

TEQUILA AMIGO

1 oz. Jose Cuervo Especial tequila
1 oz. Godiva cappuccino liqueur
1 oz. heavy cream

Layer in a shot glass.

TEQUILA BREEZE

1½ oz. Jose Cuervo Especial tequila
3 oz. pink grapefruit juice
splash club soda
lime wedge for garnish

*Shake first two ingredients well with ice and strain into a glass with ice.
Top with club soda. Garnish with a lime wedge.*

TEQUILA CANYON

1½ oz. tequila
¼ oz. triple sec
3 oz. cranberry juice
½ oz. pineapple juice
½ oz. orange juice

Pour into a glass over ice and stir.

TEQUILA COFFEE POPPER

¼ oz. tequila
¼ oz. Kahlua
7UP

Pour first two ingredients into a rocks glass and fill with 7UP. Cover glass with napkin, hold glass by rim, drop on counter and drink immediately.

TEQUILA DAISY

1½ oz. tequila
2 tsp. lemon juice
¼ oz. raspberry syrup
dash Grand Marnier
fresh fruit for garnish
mint sprig for garnish

Shake first three ingredients well (without ice). Pour into a cocktail glass with shaved ice. Stir with a spoon. Float Grand Marnier on top. Garnish with fruits and a sprig of mint.

TEQUILA FIRE "33"

3 oz. tequila
3 drops Tabasco
club soda to fill

Stir first two ingredients in a highball glass and add club soda to put out the fire.

TEQUILA FIZZ

2 oz. tequila
1 tbsp. lemon juice
¾ oz. grenadine
½ oz. lime juice
ginger ale to fill

Shake first four ingredients with ice and strain into a Collins glass over ice cubes. Fill with ginger ale and stir.

TEQUILA FROST

1¼ oz. tequila
1¼ oz. pineapple juice
1¼ oz. grapefruit juice
½ oz. honey
½ oz. grenadine
2 oz. vanilla ice cream
orange slice for garnish
cherry for garnish

Blend until smooth and pour into a parfait glass. Garnish with an orange slice and a cherry.

TEQUILA JULEP

1¼ oz. Buen Amigo tequila
1 tsp. superfine sugar
2 sprigs fresh mint
club soda to top

Crush 3 mint leaves with sugar in a chilled highball glass and fill with ice. Add Buen Amigo tequila and top with club soda. Garnish with a sprig of mint.

TEQUILA MANHATTAN

2 oz. tequila
1 oz. sweet vermouth
splash lime juice
orange slice for garnish
cherry for garnish

*Shake with ice and strain into an old-fashioned glass over ice cubes.
Garnish with a slice of orange and a cherry.*

TEQUILA MATADOR

1½ oz. Oro Azul blanco tequila
3 oz. pineapple juice
juice of ½ lime

*Shake all ingredients in a cocktail shaker with ice. Strain into a champagne
flute and serve.*

TEQUILA MOCKINGBIRD

1½ oz. tequila
1 oz. white crème de menthe
1 oz. lime juice or juice of half a lime

Shake well with ice and strain into a cocktail glass.

TEQUILA MOJITO

1½ oz. Oro Azul blanco tequila
3 oz. fresh lime juice
2 sugar cubes
1–2 fresh basil leaves

Grind the basil leaves and sugar cubes in a cocktail shaker. Add tequila and lime juice, shake until blended, and pour into a Collins glass with ice.

TEQUILA OLD-FASHIONED

1½ oz. tequila
1 splash of carbonated water
½ tsp. sugar
dash bitters
pineapple stick for garnish

Mix sugar, bitters, and 1 tsp. water in an old-fashioned glass. Add tequila, ice cubes and carbonated water. Garnish with a stick of pineapple.

TEQUILA PAINKILLER

1 oz. Jose Cuervo Especial tequila
1 oz. Smirnoff Red Label vodka
1 oz. light rum
2 oz. pineapple juice
1 oz. orange juice
½ oz. cream of coconut
pineapple slice for garnish

Blend until smooth and pour into a glass over ice. Garnish with a slice of pineapple.

TEQUILA PARALYZER

1 oz. tequila
1 oz. Kahlua
splash milk
Coca-Cola to fill
cream to taste

Build first three ingredients in a highball glass and add cream to taste. Fill with Coca-Cola.

TEQUILA PINK

1½ oz. tequila
1 oz. dry vermouth
dash grenadine

Shake with ice. Serve in a cocktail glass.

TEQUILA ROSIE

6 oz. tequila
9 oz. half-and-half or cream
2 oz. strawberry syrup (preferably Hershey's strawberry syrup)

Mix well and pour into a 25 oz. bottle. Drink will keep up to two weeks in the refrigerator.

TEQUILA SMOOTHEE

1½ oz. Cuervo gold tequila
½ oz. Grand Marnier
¾ oz. blue curaçao
½ banana
1½ oz. strawberry mix
lime wedge for garnish

Blend and pour into a sugar-rimmed glass. Garnish with a wedge of lime.

TEQUILA SOUR

1½ oz. tequila
2 oz. lemon juice
1 tsp. sugar
red cherry for garnish

Blend with crushed ice and strain into a sour glass. Garnish with a red cherry. Use anejo for a better taste.

TEQUILA SUNRISE

2 oz. ice-cold tequila
4 oz. orange juice
¼ oz. grenadine (or less if you prefer)

Pour orange juice into a highball glass and then pour in the ice-cold tequila slowly, tilting the glass to get a layered effect. Trickle grenadine on top. This should result in a perfect sunrise. Garnish with a stirrer, straw and cherry-orange. Instead of ice-cold tequila you can use ice cubes.

TEQUILA SUNSET

1 part ice-cold tequila
2 parts grapefruit juice
1 part grenadine
grapefruit slice or cherry for garnish

Pour grapefruit juice into a highball glass and then pour in the ice-cold tequila slowly, tilting the glass for a layered effect. Trickle grenadine on top. This should result in a perfect sunset. Garnish with a stirrer, straw, and grapefruit slice or cherry. Instead of ice-cold tequila you can use ice cubes.

TEQUILA TEASER

1½ oz. Buen Amigo tequila
½ oz. triple sec
1½ oz. orange juice
½ oz. grapefruit juice

Pour into tall glass over ice.

TEQUILIBRIO

1 oz. Reserva del Señor almendrado tequila
1 oz. Reserva del Señor silver tequila
1 oz. orange juice
1 oz. lemon juice
1 oz. grapefruit
pineapple slice for garnish

Serve in a tall glass. Garnish with a pineapple slice.

TEQUILINI (ORIGINAL)

2 oz. Casa Noble tequila crystal or gold
Few drops dry vermouth
¼ oz. fresh lime juice

Shake with ice and strain into a cocktail glass.

TEQUINI

1½ oz. premium silver tequila
½ oz. dry vermouth
lime twist or jalapeño-stuffed olive for garnish

A premium tequila will give any vodka or gin competition in this upscale Mexican martini. Briefly stir tequila and vermouth over cracked ice in a mixing glass until chilled. Strain ice and pour immediately into a chilled 3-oz. martini glass. Garnish with a twist of lime peel or a jalapeño-stuffed olive.

TEQUONIC

2 oz. tequila
juice of ½ lemon
tonic water to fill

Pour tequila into an old-fashioned glass and add lemon juice. Fill with tonic water and stir.

TEXAS

1 oz. Dos Manos 100 percent reposado tequila
½ oz. Gvori vodka or Brokers gin
jalapeño-stuffed olive for garnish

Shake with ice and strain into a martini glass. Garnish with a jalapeño-stuffed olive.

TEXAS TEA

½ oz. tequila
½ oz. vodka
½ oz. gin
½ oz. light rum
1 oz. pineapple juice
1 oz. Sprite
3 drops Tabasco
½ pineapple wheel for garnish

Pour into a 12-oz. highball glass packed with ice. Garnish with ½ pineapple wheel.

TEZÓN BAJA GOLD

1 oz. Tezón blanco tequila
½ oz. fresh lime juice
½ oz. simple syrup
Mexican beer
pinch salt
lime peel for garnish

Mix first three ingredients with ice and strain into a 14-oz. glass. Top with Mexican beer and add a pinch of salt. Garnish with a lime peel.

TEZÓN MARGARITA

1½ oz. Tezón reposado tequila
1 oz. Cointreau orange liqueur
1 oz. fresh lime juice
lime slice for garnish

Shake well with ice and strain into a chilled cocktail glass with a salted rim. Garnish with a lime slice. Yet another margarita, different tequila.

TEZÓN PALOMA

1½ oz. Tezón blanco tequila
½ oz. lime juice
grapefruit juice or Squirt to fill

Mix first two ingredients and pour into a tall glass over ice. Fill with grapefruit juice or Squirt.

THREE BUFFALOES

1 oz. tequila
1 oz. rum
1 oz. whisky

Mix over ice in a lowball glass.

TIJUANA TAXI

2 oz. gold tequila
1 oz. blue curaçao
1 oz. tropical fruit schnapps
lemon-lime soda
orange slice for garnish
cherry for garnish

Build first three ingredients in a highball glass and fill with lemon-lime soda. Garnish with an orange slice and a cherry.

TIJUANA TEA

¾ oz. Don Alvaro tequila
¾ Buen Amigo tequila
½ oz. triple sec
1 oz. sweet and sour mix
3 oz. Coca-Cola
lime slice for garnish
cherry for garnish

Stir. Garnish with a lime slice and a cherry.

TINGLER

1 oz. tequila (silver or white)
Tabasco salt (recipe follows)
¾ oz. Limoncello
¾ oz. Orangecello
½ oz. fresh lime juice
1 oz. simple syrup
lime slice for garnish

For the Tabasco salt: Mix 1 cup of kosher salt with 1 tbsp. Tabasco. Spread out on a plate and let dry overnight. Alternatively, spread on a baking sheet and bake for 10 minutes at 225 degrees. The salt should be free-running. Rim a martini glass with Tabasco salt.

Shake with ice and pour into a rimmed martini glass. Garnish with a lime slice.

TOMAHAWK

1 oz. tequila
1 oz. De Kuyper orange/orange liqueur
2 oz. pineapple juice
2 oz. cranberry juice
pineapple slice for garnish

Shake with cubed ice and strain. Garnish with a pineapple slice.

TOP SHELF LONG ISLAND

¼ oz. Cîroc vodka
¼ oz. Don Julio blanco tequila
¼ oz. Captain Morgan's original spiced rum
¼ oz. Tanqueray London dry gin
¼ oz. Grand Marnier
splash sweet and sour mix
1 oz. cola

Shake with ice and pour into a tall glass.

TOREADOR

1½ oz. tequila
½ oz. crème de cacao
1½ oz. light cream
whipped cream for garnish
cocoa for sprinkling

Shake with ice and strain into a cocktail glass. Garnish with whipped cream and a sprinkle of cocoa.

TRAFFIC LIGHT COOLER

¾ oz. melon liqueur (green)
1 oz. gold tequila (green)
splash sour mix (yellow)
2 oz. orange juice (yellow)
½ oz. sloe gin (red)
cherry for garnish
lemon and lime slices for garnish

Layer in a cordial glass. Garnish with a cherry and lemon and lime slices.

TROJAN BOMBER

1 oz. Jose Cuervo tequila
1 oz. Crown Royal
1 can 7UP
juice of ½ lemon
Tabasco (optional for flavor)

Pour the 7UP over ice in a highball glass. In a shaker, shake the whisky and the tequila and pour into the highball glass. Stir in the lemon juice and serve.

TROPICAL

1½ oz. Buen Amigo tequila
3 oz. orange juice
1 tsp. lemon juice
½ oz. grenadine
½ orange slice for garnish
cherry for garnish

Mix in highball glass with cracked ice. Garnish with half an orange slice and a cherry.

TRUFFLE CREAM CAFE

1½ oz. Tequila Rose—java
hot coffee
whipped cream to top
chocolate syrup for drizzling

Pour tequila into a preheated mug. Fill with hot coffee. Garnish with whipped cream and chocolate syrup drizzle.

VAMPIRO

2 oz. XXX tequila
Chilled sangrita
dash orange or grapefruit juice
salt to rim glass
lemon wedge
lemon slice for garnish

Wipe the lemon wedge over the rim of a tall highball glass to moisten it, then dip the rim into the salt. Place a few ice cubes in the glass and pour in XXX tequila. Add the orange or grapefruit juice and top off with sangrita. Garnish with a lemon slice.

VANILLA SUNSET

1 oz. Jose Cuervo tequila
1 oz. Dr. McGillicuddy's vanilla liqueur
4 drops Tabasco
cranberry juice to fill

Mix first three ingredients in a glass and top with cranberry juice.

VERTIGO

1¼ oz. Buen Amigo tequila
2 oz. sweet and sour mix
1 oz. cranberry juice
juice of ½ lemon
orange wheel for garnish

Stir. Garnish with an orange wheel.

VETERAN

1½ oz. anejo tequila
1½ oz. Kahlua
½ oz. triple sec

Serve at room temperature or warmed in a snifter glass.

VIVA VILLA

1½ oz. tequila
Juice of 1 lime
1 tsp. sugar
lemon juice to rim glass
salt to rim glass

Rub the rim of an old-fashioned glass with lemon juice and dip in salt.
Shake with ice and strain into the salt-rimmed glass over ice cubes.

VODKALOO

1 oz. silver tequila
1 oz. Smirnoff vodka
1 oz. beer
1 oz. Coca-Cola

Serve in a tall glass with lots of ice.

VOLCANO

1 oz. tequila
1 oz. vodka
1 oz. Jim Beam bourbon whisky
1 oz. gin
1 oz. rum
3 oz. orange juice
3 oz. pineapple juice
splash grenadine
7UP to fill

Pour first five ingredients into a quart jar over ice. Add juices and grenadine. Fill with 7UP.

WABORITA

2 oz. Cabo Wabo tequila
2 oz. Cointreau
2 oz. fresh lime juice

Shake with ice and strain into a salt-rimmed martini glass. Garnish with a lime slice. Another with Cabo Wabo!

WABORITA #2

2 oz. Cabo Wabo reposado tequila
2 oz. fresh lime juice
1 oz. triple sec
splash blue curaçao
lime slice for garnish

Shake with ice and strain into a salt-rimmed martini glass. Garnish with a lime slice. Another with Cabo Wabo!

WALKING HOME

1 oz. Jose Cuervo tequila
1 oz. vodka
1 oz. rum
juice of 2 limes
½ oz. sloe gin
dash maraschino cherry juice

Mix first four ingredients with ice and strain into a glass. Add a dash of cherry juice for color.

WARM BLONDE

Equal parts:
XXX tequila
Southern Comfort
amaretto

Layer in a pony glass or a shot glass.

WATERMELON MARGARITA

1½ oz. Patron silver tequila
2 oz. fresh-pressed watermelon juice
1 oz. juice of one small lime, hand extracted
1 oz. fresh lemon sour
¾ oz. Patron Citronge
watermelon spear for garnish

Shake with ice until well blended and strain into a 14-oz. goblet over ice. Garnish with a spear of watermelon.

WENG-WENG

¾ oz. tequila
¾ oz. vodka
¾ oz. brandy
¾ oz. bourbon
¾ oz. scotch whisky
¾ oz. rum
Equal parts:
orange juice
pineapple juice
dash grenadine

Mix first six ingredients in a Collins glass. Add ice cubes up to ¾ of glass. Stir. Fill in with equal portions of chilled orange and pineapple juices to top. Add a dash of grenadine.

WEST COAST PARALYZER

1 oz. tequila
1 oz. Kahlua
½ glass milk
½ glass root beer

Build over ice in a Collins glass.

WET SPOT

1 oz. tequila
2 oz. Irish cream

Serve in a rocks glass over ice.

WHITE BULL

¾ oz. Oro Azul reposado tequila
¾ oz. Kahlua
cream to fill

Shake first two ingredients with ice until blended and pour into a high-ball glass over ice. Fill with cream to taste. Everyone likes to mix with Kahlua and cream.

WHITE CACTUS

1 oz. tequila
ginger ale to taste
splash lime juice

Pour into a highball glass over ice and garnish with a slice of lime. Many cocktails with tequila and ginger ale. Different names!

THE WHITE DEVIL

¾ oz. Cuervo gold tequila
¾ oz. Crown Royal
3 dashes Tabasco (for glass rim)
margarita salt (for glass rim)
lime wedge for garnish

Take a rocks glass and turn it sideways. Put a few dashes of Tabasco pepper sauce on the rim of the glass and turn until pepper sauce has encircled the rim. Put glass into margarita salt. Pour into Tabasco- and salt-rimmed glass and garnish with a lime wedge.

WHITE MEXICAN

1 oz. tequila
1 oz. Irish cream
½ oz. crème de cacao
dash peppermint schnapps
half-and-half or cream to top

Pour first four ingredients into a highball glass over ice and top with half-and-half.

WIKI WAKI WOO

½ oz. tequila
½ oz. vodka
½ oz. rum
½ oz. Bacardi 151 proof rum
½ oz. triple sec
1 oz. amaretto
1 oz. orange juice
1 oz. pineapple juice
1 oz. cranberry juice
orange slice for garnish
cherry for garnish

Mix with ice and pour into a hurricane or parfait glass. Garnish with an orange slice and a cherry. Use a very tall glass.

WILD LOVE

1 shot tequila
½ shot white rum
1½ shots De Kuyper wild strawberry
½ shot lemon juice
orange juice
fresh strawberry for garnish

Build the first four ingredients in a highball glass with cubed ice. Top with orange juice. Garnish with a fresh strawberry cut in half.

WILD ROSE

2 part Tequila Rose
2 part McCormick Irish cream
1 part Polar Ice vodka

Shake well and serve on the rocks.

WILD THING

1½ oz. tequila
1 oz. cranberry juice
1 oz. club soda
½ oz. lime juice

Pour over ice into an old-fashioned glass. Garnish with a lime wedge.

WINE AND DINE MARGARITA

6 oz. tequila
3 oz. triple sec
1 can margarita mix (preferably the frozen Bacardi margarita mixer)
3 oz. water
1 oz. sangria
sugar to rim glass

Blend the first four ingredients with ice. Pour the sangria into a cocktail glass rimmed with sugar and top with the blended mixture. Makes three cocktails.

WISH YOU WERE HERE

2 oz. tequila
1 oz. lemon liqueur
litchi juice to fill

Pour first two ingredients into a glass and top with litchi juice. Garnish with a wedge of lime, squeeze, and throw in after first sip.

THE WOOLY MAMMOTH

1 oz. tequila
1 oz. Archers (available in England now)
1 oz. Malibu rum
1 oz. Bacardi rum
1 oz. lime cordial
lemonade to fill

Pour first five ingredients into a cocktail shaker and fill with lemonade. Shake with ice and strain into a highball glass. Drink slowly through a straw.

WORLD'S BEST FROZEN BLUE MARGARITA

1½ oz. Tarantula Azul tequila
4½ oz. Tarantula Azul margarita mix
salt to rim glass

Blend with ice and serve in a salt-rimmed margarita glass.

THE WRECK

2 oz. Oro Azul reposado tequila
2 oz. melon liqueur
2 oz. cranberry juice
1 oz. Jagermeister

Shake with ice until blended and pour into a Collins glass.

XO NIGHT CAP

½ oz. Patron XO Café tequila
½ oz. Baileys Original Irish cream
⅓ oz. Jagermeister
⅓ oz. Goldschlager
1 oz. half-and-half
cinnamon sugar to rim glass

Shake and strain into a 7 ½-oz. stem glass rimmed with cinnamon sugar.

X-TINA'S CINNAMON FIREBALL

3 parts tequila
1 part cinnamon schnapps
1 part club soda
1 part Coca-Cola
8 dashes Tabasco

Chill and pour into a shot glass. Garnish with a cinnamon stick.

XXX

2 oz. XXX tequila
1 oz. orange juice
3 oz. pomegranate juice (Pom Wonderful)

Serve on the rocks. or shake vigorously with cracked ice in a stainless steel shaker and strain into a broad-bowled, stemmed cocktail glass.

XXX BREEZE

2 oz. XXX tequila
3 oz. grapefruit juice
club soda to top

Mix first two ingredients with ice. Pour into a rocks glass and top with club soda.

XXX CAFE

2 oz. Patron XO Café tequila
coffee ice cream
1 tsp. finely ground coffee beans
freshly grated nutmeg for dusting

Blend as a very thick malt shake. Pour into chilled cocktail glasses and dust with freshly grated nutmeg.

XXX COOLER

2 oz. XXX tequila
2 oz. Cuarenta y Tres (Liquor 43)
seltzer or club soda to top

Stir first two ingredients in a rocks glass three-fourths full of ice cubes. Top with seltzer or club soda. Stir well.

XXXONIC

2 parts XXX tequila
chilled tonic water to fill
¼ lime
coarse salt to rim glass
lime slices for garnish

Rub the rim of a tall highball glass with ¼ lime and then dip the rim into a bowl of coarse salt to coat it lightly. Fill glass with ice and squeeze in remaining lime juice. Add XXX tequila and stir. Fill with tonic water. Garnish with lime slices.

XXXTASY

2 parts XXX tequila
1½ parts dry vermouth
1½ parts sweet vermouth
maraschino cherry for garnish

Shake well with ice and strain into a chilled martini glass. Garnish with a maraschino cherry.

YELLOW BOXER

1¾ oz. tequila
¼ oz. Galliano herbal liqueur
¾ oz. orange juice
¾ oz. Rose's lime juice
¾ oz. lemon juice

Shake well over ice and strain into a chilled cocktail glass.

THE YELLOW ROSE OF TEXAS

1½ oz. Gran Centenario Plata tequila
3 oz. yellow tomato puree (puree yellow tomatoes and strain through
   a china cap; discard anything left in china cap)
½ oz. lemon juice
⅛ tsp. ground cumin
¼ tsp. kosher salt
5 dashes Tabasco habanero sauce
chili powder, salt, and sugar to rim glass
lemon wheel for garnish

Rim glass with equal parts mixture of chili powder, salt, and sugar. Shake with ice and strain into the rimmed and chilled cocktail glass. Garnish with a lemon wheel.

YUCATAN-STYLE SANGRIA

1½ oz. Don Julio anejo tequila
1 28-oz. can tomatoes
8 oz. orange juice
¼ oz. lime juice
1 slice white onion
1 seeded green chile
1 tsp. sugar
¼ tsp. hot pepper sauce
lime wedge for garnish

Blend all ingredients except tequila until smooth and pour enough to fill a tequila shot glass. Add Don Julio anejo tequila to another tequila shot glass. Garnish with a lime wedge.

YVETTE

2 oz. tequila
1 oz. apricot brandy
2 oz. cream
Sprite

Mix first three ingredients in a highball glass and fill with Sprite.

ZIPPER

1½ oz. Cointreau
1½ oz. tequila
½ oz. cream

Layer in a lowball glass.

ZIPPY MARGARITA

2 oz. Cuervo tequila
1½ oz. blue curaçao
½ oz. Courvoisier
3 drops Tabasco
4 oz. sour mix
Hungarian pepper for garnish

Rim 13-oz. poco glass with salt and pepper. Blend with ice, then pour into poco glass rimmed with salt and pepper and garnish with an orange wedge. Cut tip off of a Hungarian pepper and use as garnish. Serve frozen.

ZIPOLETION

10 fresh raspberries
1¼ oz. Patron silver
splash Patron citronge
juice of ¼ lime
orange slice for garnish

Muddle raspberries and Patron silver. Shake muddled mixture and the remaining ingredients with ice and strain into a chilled martini glass. Garnish with a fresh orange slice.

50

FOOD RECIPES
USING TEQUILA

TEQUILA CHICKEN FETTUCCINE

2 oz. Pepe Lopez tequila
3 tbsp. butter
¼ cup cilantro, roughly chopped
2 tbsp. minced garlic
2 tbsp. jalapeño, finely chopped and seeded
½ cup chicken stock
2 tbsp. lime juice
¼ onion, peeled and sliced
1¼ lb. skinless chicken breast, cubed
1½ cups heavy whipping cream
1 lb. fettuccine, cooked

In a medium skillet, heat 2 tbsp. of the butter and sauté the cilantro, garlic, and jalapeno for 4–5 minutes, stirring frequently to prevent scorching. Add the chicken stock, tequila, and lime juice, and cook until the mixture is reduced by half. Set aside. In another skillet, melt the remaining butter, sauté the onion until soft, add the chicken, and cook, stirring, until cooked through. Add the tequila mixture and cream and toss with the hot pasta. Serves 4.

TEQUILA MARINADE FOR STEAK

3 parts Pepe Lopez tequila
1 part Worcestershire sauce
dash hot sauce
salt to taste
fresh ground pepper to taste

Combine ingredients and use to marinate steak. If possible, marinate overnight.

PEPE'S TIPSY SWEET POTATOES

¼ cup Pepe Lopez tequila
¼ cup butter
1¼ pounds sweet potatoes, roughly grated
3 tbsp. brown sugar
¼ tsp. salt
juice of 2 limes

Preheat oven to 220°F. Mix 2 tbsp. brown sugar, the salt, and the sweet potatoes together. In an oven-safe baking dish, pat down mixture into one even layer. Sprinkle remaining brown sugar over top. Bake for one hour. Remove from oven and stir in 3 tbsp. tequila and the juice of one lime. Pat mixture back down and continue baking the potatoes another 50 minutes, until tender. Remove from oven, stir in remaining tequila and lime juice, and serve warm. Serves 4.

PEPE'S PEPPY WINGS

½ cup Pepe Lopez tequila
2 lbs. precut chicken wings
¼ cup frozen orange juice concentrate
grated zest of 1 lemon

juice of 1 lemon
2 garlic cloves, minced
½ tsp. ground cumin
1 tsp. black pepper
1 tsp. salt
2 tsp. cilantro, minced

Wash the wings, pat dry gently, and place in a large, resealable plastic bag. In a small bowl, combine the remaining ingredients. Pour over the wings in the bag, making sure to completely coat the wings. Seal the bag and refrigerate several hours or overnight. Prepare a medium-hot charcoal fire or preheat a gas grill to medium-high. Drain the wings, discarding any leftover juices from the marinade. Grill the wings, turning often, until they are slightly charred and cooked through, about 25 minutes. Serves 4.

TEQUILA LIME PIE

½ cup Pepe Lopez tequila
1 pie crust, baked
8 eggs
8 egg yolks
1½ cup sugar
¾ cup fresh-squeezed lime juice
zest of 1 lime
9 tbsp. unsalted butter, cut into small pieces
sweetened whipped cream, to serve

Mix eggs, yolks, sugar, lime juice, lime zest, and tequila in a stainless-steel bowl. Whip constantly with a whisk over a simmering pot of water until thick (about 15 minutes). Mixture should be jelly-like. Remove bowl from simmering water and add pieces of butter. Beat until melted. Pour into baked pie crust and refrigerate at least 4 hours, or overnight. Serve with sweetened whipped cream. Makes one pie; serves 6.

GRILLED TEQUILA LIME CHICKEN

½ cup Pepe Lopez tequila
½ cup fresh lime juice
½ cup orange juice
¼ cup fresh cilantro, chopped
2 tbsp. jalapeño chilies, minced and seeded
1¼ tbsp. chili powder
1 tsp. salt
¾ tsp. ground black pepper
6 boneless chicken breast halves with skin
oil for brushing grill

Mix first 8 ingredients in a bowl. Add chicken; turn to coat. Cover; chill overnight. Prepare barbecue grill (medium heat). Brush grill rack with oil. Grill chicken until cooked through, turning occasionally, about 18 minutes. Serve with Tropical Fruit Salsa (recipe follows). Serves 6.

TROPICAL FRUIT SALSA

¼ cup Pepe Lopez tequila
1 cup pineapple, peeled and finely diced
½ cup mango, firm-ripe, peeled and finely diced
⅓ cup red onion, finely chopped
3 tbsp. fresh cilantro, chopped
1 tbsp. fresh orange juice
1 tbsp. fresh lime juice
½ tsp. minced fresh jalapeño chili, including seeds
½ tsp. salt

Stir all ingredients together.

GARDEN GAZPACHO

¼ cup Pepe Lopez tequila
1 lb. large tomatoes
1 large cucumber, peeled, halved lengthwise, and seeded
1 medium onion
1 roasted bell pepper, large, in jar
3 cups tomato juice
½ cup fresh cilantro, chopped
½ cup fresh-squeezed lime juice
⅓ cup rice wine or apple cider vinegar
¼ cup olive oil
⅛ tsp. hot pepper sauce

Cut 1 tomato, ½ cucumber, and ½ onion into 1-inch pieces and transfer to processor. Add bell pepper and puree. Transfer to bowl. Add tomato juice, cilantro, vinegar, tequila, oil, and hot pepper sauce. Seed remaining tomatoes. Dice remaining tomatoes and cucumber and onion halves and add to soup. Season with salt and pepper. Refrigerate. Can be prepared 2 days ahead of serving. Serve well chilled.

GUAVA GLAZED PORK TENDERLOIN

4 oz. Pepe Lopez tequila
1 tbsp. vegetable oil
1 tbsp. onion, minced
1 clove garlic, minced
7 oz. guava paste, chopped
½ cup water
1 tbsp. soy sauce
1 tbsp. ketchup
1 tsp. cayenne pepper
Salt to taste
2¾ lb. pork tenderloins
2 cilantro sprigs

To make the glazed pork: Heat the oil in a small saucepan. Add the onion and garlic and cook over moderate heat, stirring, until softened. Reduce the heat to low. Add the guava paste and water and cook, stirring, until the paste has dissolved. Stir in the tequila, soy sauce, ketchup, and cayenne. Season with salt. Set the pork tenderloins in a 9-by-13-inch glass baking dish and brush them all over with half the guava glaze. Light a fire or heat a grill pan over moderate heat. Grill the pork, turning and brushing with the remaining glaze, until browned on all sides and cooked to internal temperature of 150°F. Transfer the pork to a cutting board and let rest 15 minutes.

To make the salsa: In a bowl, mix the cilantro, oil, chives, jalapeños, and garlic. Season with salt.

Thinly slice the pork. Garnish with cilantro sprigs, and serve with the salsa. Serves 4.

ASS KICKIN' CACTUS

1½ oz. tequila (preferably Jose Cuervo)
4–6 dashes any flavor Tabasco
3 fresh jalapeño peppers, large
1–2 oz. chunky peanut butter
margarita salt, as needed
2 edible flowers
½ oz. julienne fried potatoes
1 tbsp. diced red and yellow peppers

Remove tips of jalapeños so they are at different heights. Remove seeds and pith while leaving the stem end intact and without making any holes (to prevent leakage).

Place the peanut butter on a plate. Rim the jalapeño peppers with salt and place on the peanut butter. Fill each pepper with the tequila and add a dash or two of your favorite Tabasco sauce.

Garnish with the fried potatoes for the dry creek bed and with the peppers and flowers around the potatoes.

Drink the tequila.

Then take a knife and cut the peppers in half lengthwise and fill with the peanut butter and enjoy eating them.

YARD BIRD MCILHENNY W/CORN FIRED RAVIOLI IN A TEQUILA JALAPEÑO SAUCE

For chicken:
3 cups cornmeal
1¾ cups flour, all-purpose
6 tbsp. paprika (preferably hot)
3 oz. Tabasco
6 large eggs, scrambled
12 4-oz. boneless chicken breast halves, lightly pounded

For sauce:
6 lbs. fresh plum tomatoes, or 1 #10 can dried
salt to taste
olive oil (enough to coat tomatoes)
1½ lbs. butter
4½ cups tequila
1½ qt. heavy cream
4 oz. Tabasco green pepper sauce
3 cups grated Parmesan

To prepare the chicken breast:
Mix cornmeal, ¾ cup flour (reserving 1 cup), and paprika. Mix Tabasco and eggs. Set aside. Clean and pound out chicken breast. Coat chicken in one cup reserved flour, then egg wash, then cornmeal mixture. Set aside.

To make the sauce:
Slice tomatoes in half lengthwise and put on sheet pan, cut side up. Salt and drizzle with oil. Bake at 375°F until they collapse. Puree tomatoes in processor (do not overpuree). Set aside.

To assemble sauce, melt butter in sauce pan, add tequila, bring to a boil and simmer 2–3 minutes, stirring gently. Add heavy cream, bring back to a boil, and simmer another 2–3 minutes, stirring gently. Add the pureed tomatoes and Tabasco green pepper sauce. Bring to a boil and simmer 2–3 minutes, stirring gently. Take off heat, stir to cool slightly, mix in grated cheese, and hold.

To prepare the ravioli:
Boil, drain, and coat in flour. Dip into the egg wash and coat in cornmeal as per the chicken breast and fry off. Hold.

To assemble the dish:
Preheat oven to 350°F. Spread a little sauce onto a sheet pan and put cooked chicken breast on top of sauce. With the back of a ladle, spread a thin coat of sauce on top of each breast. Arrange mozzarella on top of roasted pepper in attractive manner. Put into the oven to melt the cheese. When cheese is melted, place one chicken breast onto a warm plate, arrange fried ravioli next to chicken, ladle sauce over, and garnish with parsley.

TIPSY TABASCO SORBET

For sorbet:
Juice of 10 limes
3 tsp. Tabasco green pepper sauce
½ cup sugar
¼ cup water
zest of 3 limes
½ bunch cilantro

For grilled fruits:
tequila, for garnish
1 pineapple
1 papaya
1 avocado
⅛ cup macadamia oil

3 tsp. Tabasco
1 pinch sea salt
¼ tsp. curry powder

Bring lime juice, Tabasco green pepper sauce, sugar, and water to a boil. Remove mixture from heat, let cool. Add lime zest and cilantro. Put mixture in sorbet or ice cream machine until frozen.

Wash and slice grilled fruits. Add macadamia oil, Tabasco, and sea salt. To pineapple only, add curry powder. Heat grill, sear and mark fruit. Remove from heat and bring to room temperature.

To serve, plate grilled fruits along with sorbet. Drizzle tequila over platter and sprinkle with sea salt.

TIAJUANA PESTO SALSA

3 tbsp. tequila
2 cups fully prepared pesto
½ cup Bermuda onion, finely diced
½ cup red pepper, finely diced
1 cup cucumber, seeded and finely diced
¾ cup pine nuts, roasted
1¾ cups Tabasco green pepper sauce
½ cup chopped cilantro, loosely packed
¼ cup lime juice

Combine all ingredients and refrigerate until ready to serve.

TEQUILA SUNRISE WINGS

2 oz. tequila
16 chicken wings, wing tips cut off and discarded and the wings
    halved at the joint
2 tbsp. canola oil
1 tsp. salt
4 oz. orange juice

2 tbsp. lime juice
2 tbsp. maraschino cherry juice
2 tbsp. Tabasco green pepper sauce

Combine ingredients in a bowl and reserve half. Preheat grill to medium high. Add wings to bowl and toss to coat. Grill chicken wings and baste with reserved marinade, turning once, until the juices run clear when pierced with a fork.

TEQUILA PRAWNS WITH CUCUMBER RELISH

For cucumber relish:
3 hothouse cucumbers, cut in half lengthwise, then cut into thin half
    moons (30 oz.)
¼ cup cilantro, chopped
1 tbsp. garlic, chopped
1 cup red onion, thinly sliced
3 yellow tomatoes, cut in medium dice (1¼ lbs.)
3 tbsp. olive oil
1½ tbsp. cumin, ground
4 tbsp. Tabasco green pepper sauce
juice of 2 lemons
salt and pepper, to taste

For tequila shrimp:
8 oz. tequila
72 raw shrimp, peeled, deveined (7 lbs.)
¼ cup cilantro, chopped
½ cup Tabasco green pepper sauce
1 cup olive oil
juice of 2 limes

For blue and red tortilla fizzles:
10 red 6-inch corn tortillas, julienned

10 blue 6-inch corn tortillas, julienned

To make cucumber relish:
Mix first 10 ingredients in a bowl, cover, and refrigerate until ready to use. Marinate shrimp with tequila, cilantro, Tabasco green pepper sauce, olive oil, and lime juice; refrigerate for 1–2 hours.

To prepare shrimp and blue and red tortilla fizzles:
Grill or sauté shrimp over medium-high heat for 1–1½ minutes on each side. Fry tortilla strips until crisp, drain, and set aside.

To assemble:
For each serving, place a 6-oz. mound of cucumber relish in center of plate. Arrange 4 shrimp around the cucumber relish. Top with ½ oz. of the tortilla frizzles.

TEQUILA-MARINATED GRILLED PORK CHOPS WITH TANGY PEANUT SAUCE

For pork chops:
2 tbsp. tequila
4 cloves garlic, minced
2 tbsp. ginger, chopped
2 tsp. lime zest, grated
1 cup lime juice
2 tbsp. honey
2 tbsp. Tabasco
12 6-8 oz. boneless pork chops, butterflied

For tangy peanut sauce:
2 cloves garlic, minced
1 tbsp. ginger, grated
2 green onions, finely chopped
1 tsp. lime zest, grated
1½ tbsp. Tabasco

¼ cup smooth peanut butter
¼ cup fresh lime juice
1 tbsp. honey

To prepare pork chops:
Mix garlic and ginger and place in a flat glass dish. Add the lime zest, lime juice, honey, Tabasco, and tequila. Pierce pork chops with fork and marinate at least 1 hour, turning frequently until ready to grill.

Heat grill until very hot. Cook chops about six inches from heat source for 5 minutes, turn, and brush with peanut sauce. Cook for 5 minutes and turn. Cook for 2 minutes longer or to an internal temperature of 160°F.

To make tangy peanut sauce:
Mix garlic and ginger together. Add green onions and lime zest. In a blender or mixer, combine Tabasco, smooth peanut butter, lime juice, and honey. Stir into the ginger and garlic combination. Brush onto grilled pork chops before serving. Serves 12.

TABASCO AND LIME CHICKEN BREASTS AND JALAPEÑO RICE

For chicken:
10 12-oz. chicken breasts
Salt and pepper to taste

For marinade:
12 oz. tequila
1 head garlic, finely minced
1 large onion, julienne
10 limes, sliced
5 jalapeño peppers, seeded, deveined, and finely diced
1 bunch oregano, finely chopped
1 bunch thyme, finely chopped
12 oz. Tabasco green pepper sauce

12 oz. white wine vinegar
108 oz. olive oil

For rice:
8 oz. butter
2 onions, finely diced
8 jalapeño peppers, seeded, finely diced
1 red bell pepper, seeded, finely diced
4 cups rice
12 oz. Tabasco green pepper sauce
2 qts. vegetable stock
½ bunch fresh oregano, finely chopped
Fresh ground pepper to taste
2½ cups finely grated jalapeño jack cheese

Clean and remove all the fat from the chicken breasts. Season with salt and pepper. Set aside in hotel pan. Mix all the ingredients for the marinade. Pour the marinade over the chicken breasts. Let marinate in the refrigerator for at least 2 to 4 hours. After the chicken is finished marinating, preheat the grill. Grill the chicken to desired doneness, being careful not to overcook and dry out chicken. Slice the chicken on the bias and serve on the jalapeño rice (directions follow).

In a saucepan, melt the butter and sauté the onions until translucent. Add the jalapeños and bell pepper. Sauté until softened. Add the rice and sauté for 2 minutes. Then add the Tabasco green pepper sauce and vegetable stock. Bring to a boil. Cover and simmer for 20 minutes. Check the rice for doneness. Cook until all liquid has been absorbed. Stir in the oregano and black pepper. Place ½ cup of rice in a ring mold, place on plate, and remove the ring. Place 1 oz. of cheese on top of rice and melt under broiler. Serves 20.

GRILLED RIB EYES WITH CHILE-LIME-TEQUILA BUTTER

6 rib eye steaks

Olive oil as needed
Chile-lime-tequila compound butter, enough to slice into 6 rounds

Heat a gas or charcoal grill to a medium-hot temperature (about 350°F to 375°F). Brush both sides of steaks with oil, and season well with salt and freshly ground black pepper. Let steaks rest at room temperature at least 15 minutes before grilling.

When the grill is heated, place steaks on the grate and close the lid. After about 4 minutes, rotate steaks a quarter turn to create crosshatched marks. After another 3 to 4 minutes, flip steaks over. After another 4 minutes, rotate steaks a quarter turn and grill to desired doneness. (It will take about 15 minutes of total cooking time to reach an internal temperature of 130°F for medium rare.) Remove steaks from the grill and let rest 7 to 10 minutes before serving.

To serve, slice compound butter into 6 rounds and top each steak with a round. Serves 6.

JALAPEÑO PESTO SALSA

3 tbsp. tequila
2 cups fully prepared pesto
½ cup Bermuda onion, finely diced
½ cup red pepper, finely diced
1 cup cucumber, seeded, finely diced
¾ cup pine nuts, roasted
1¾ cups Tabasco green pepper sauce
½ cup cilantro, chopped, loose pack
¼ cup lime juice

Combine all ingredients and refrigerate until ready to serve.

DRUNKEN SKIRT STEAK

½ cup tequila

6 tbsp. lime juice
1 lime
zest of 1 lime
4 garlic cloves
1 tsp. kosher salt
3 tbsp. Tabasco chipotle pepper sauce
8 fresh mint leaves
2 lbs., 6 oz. skirt steak

Chiffon mint leaves. Small dice garlic and combine with zest from lime. Squeeze lime juice into bowl, discarding seeds. Combine all marinade ingredients. Trim fat from steak. Filet steak so that there are two pieces the same length. Cut each piece into sixths, making 12 3-oz. strips. Put strips in casserole dish and add marinade. Cover with plastic wrap and shake a few times to mix. Marinate for 3 hours.

In a hot sauté pan, or on a grill, add two to three pieces of steak at a time. Turn after one minute. Remove from heat when steak has a nice marking. Repeat with all steak strips. Do not overcook.

BAJA TABASCO SHRIMP

½ cup tequila
3 lbs. large shrimp, cleaned and deveined
1 onion, thinly sliced lengthwise
8 garlic cloves, minced
6 tbsp. olive oil
2 tbsp. Worcestershire sauce
½ cup fish or vegetable stock
2 tbsp. Tabasco green pepper sauce
1 tbsp. Tabasco chipotle pepper sauce
¼ cup fresh pineapple, diced
2 tsp. lime zest
1 pasilla pepper, roasted; seeds, skins, and veins removed
6 tomatoes, peeled and ¼-in. diced
salt and pepper to taste

12 cups rice, cooked
diced sweet peppers, for garnish

Puree peppers in a food processor with half the tomatoes and half the garlic.

In a large skillet, heat olive oil and sauté the minced garlic and onion until the onion is translucent. Add the shrimp and cook until they turn bright pink. Add the tequila, stock, pepper sauce, Worcestershire, and the rest of the tomatoes. Salt and pepper to taste.

Add the pureed sauce. Cover and simmer for 5 minutes.

Serve shrimp over rice. Place sauce on plate, then mound rice in the center. Arrange shrimp around the rice. Garnish with diced sweet peppers, diced pineapple, and Tabasco green pepper sauce.

CARIBBEAN FRUIT CHILI

3 oz. tequila
1 tbsp. garam masala
1 tbsp. chili powder
1 tbsp. Tabasco
1 cup coconut milk
½ cup brown sugar, firmly packed
½ cup fresh lime juice
½ tsp. salt
½ cup each fruit juices; combine any 3, such as peach, orange, papaya, mango, pineapple
6 cups fresh fruit, such as mango, papaya, peach, kiwi
strawberry, ½-in. cubed, for garnish
sour cream for garnish
brown sugar for garnish
fresh mint leaves for garnish

Combine fruit juices of choice, chili powder, and garam masala in a stainless steel sauce pan. Simmer for 15 minutes, and then cool in an ice-water bath.

Add Tabasco, coconut milk, brown sugar, lime juice, tequila, and salt. Add desired cubed fruits and marinate 4–24 hours.

Serve in a soup bowl or mug with a dollop of sour cream sweetened with brown sugar and fresh mint leaves.

TOUCHDOWN TEQUILA CHICKEN WITH VEGETABLE MARINADE

For vegetable marinade:
½ cup olive oil
½ cup lime juice or margarita mix
1 tsp. liquid smoke
½ tsp. kosher salt
½ tsp. freshly ground black pepper

For tequila chicken:
½ cup tequila
1¼ cups lime juice or margarita mix
½ cup triple sec or orange juice
¼ cup chopped fresh cilantro leaves
4 cloves garlic, minced
1 tsp. crushed red pepper flakes
8 boneless, skinless chicken breast halves
1 large red bell pepper, cut into thick strips
1 yellow bell pepper, cut into thick strips
1 large Vidalia onion, cut into wedges
shredded Mexican cheese blend for serving
salsa for serving
sour cream for serving

To make vegetable marinade:
Combine all ingredients into a bowl. Yields about 1 cup.

To prepare dish:

In a bowl, combine lime juice, tequila, triple sec, cilantro, garlic, and red pepper flakes. Add chicken and marinate chicken for 3 hours or overnight (depending on how much you like the tequila flavor).

Marinate peppers and onion in vegetable marinade for 30 minutes to 1 hour.

Preheat outdoor grill to medium heat. Remove chicken from marinade and grill, turning once, until juices run clear, about 5 to 6 minutes per side. Drain peppers and onions, grill in a grill basket until tender and browned on edges, about 8 to 10 minutes.

Slice the chicken breast into ½-inch strips. Serve with peppers and onions, cheese, salsa, and sour cream.

TEQUILA-SPIKED WATERMELON SOUP

For tequila syrup:
½ cup tequila
1 cup sugar
¾ cup water
¼ cup triple sec

For triple sec whipped cream:
1 cup heavy cream
2 tbsp. watermelon juice
2 tbsp. triple sec

For soup:
¼ cup tequila
3 cups watermelon, seeded and diced
2½ cups melon puree (approximately 3 cups watermelon, seeded, diced, pureed, and strained until smooth)
1½ cups tequila syrup
¼ cup melon juice
juice of 2 limes
4 tbsp. red and yellow melon, diced, for garnish

1 tbsp. triple sec
zest of 1 lime blanched in tequila syrup

To make tequila syrup:
Combine all syrup ingredients. Place on medium heat until sugar dissolves. Chill until cold.

To make triple sec whipped cream garnish:
Combine whipped cream ingredients and beat to stiff peaks. Pipe rosettes on waxed paper–lined pan. Freeze.

To make soup:
Place 3 cups of watermelon in a food processor. Pour out excess juice and reserve. Puree watermelon until smooth. In a bowl, combine the melon puree, the reserved juice, 1½ cups tequila syrup, ¼ cup tequila, and lime juice, and chill.

In another small bowl, combine 4 tbsp. diced melons for garnish, 1 tbsp. triple sec, and lime zest, and chill.

To serve, place whipped cream garnish in the bottom of a kosher-salt-rimmed bowl or glass. Pour 6 oz. of soup into the bowl or glass. Garnish with 1 tbsp. of the diced melons and sprinkle with salt.

DRUNKEN ANGEL FOOD CAKE WITH TEQUILA AND LIME

For syrup:
½ cup tequila
¼ cup lime juice
1 lime, zested and juiced
½ cup superfine sugar
pinch salt

For icing:
1 cup tequila
½ box confectioners' sugar

pinch salt
zest of 1 lime
1 cup lime juice

For cake:
store-bought angel food cake
store-bought candied lime zest
whipped cream to serve

To make syrup:
Combine all ingredients except the tequila in a saucepan and bring to a
boil, stirring constantly until the sugar has melted. Remove syrup from
heat, add the tequila, and cool to room temperature.

To make icing:
Place the sugar, salt, and lime zest in a bowl. Add the liquids a little at a
time until the mixture is just loose enough to pour. Be careful not to add
too much liquid, but if you do, add more sugar as needed.

To assemble:
Hold the cake upside down and cut a little well around the bottom of
the cake. Pour half of the syrup evenly over the cake. Turn the cake over
and, using a pastry brush, paint the cake with the remaining syrup.
Drizzle the icing over the cake. Sprinkle with candied lime zest. Slice and
serve with whipped cream.

TEQUILA CHICKEN QUESADILLAS

Main ingredients:
1 oz. tequila
3 tbsp. canola oil
1 lb. boneless, skinless chicken breast, julienned
½ tsp. kosher salt
¼ tsp. freshly ground black pepper
2 dashes cayenne pepper

1½ tbsp. cumin
1 clove garlic, minced
1 red bell pepper, julienned
1 green bell pepper, julienned
1 small red onion, thinly sliced
8 oz. Colby jack, Monterey jack, or cheddar cheese, shredded
2 tbsp. unsalted butter
2 tbsp. cilantro leaves, finely chopped
2 tbsp. sliced scallions

For all-purpose soy flour flat bread (makes 2, but only use 1 for this quesadilla recipe):
1½ cups soy flour
¼ cup sugar substitute (preferably Splenda)
½ tsp. salt
3 eggs
¾ cup heavy cream
⅓ cup club soda
nonstick vegetable oil cooking spray

Special equipment:
2 12-inch round aluminum pizza pans

To make soy flour flat bread:
Preheat oven to 375°F.

In a medium bowl, whisk together the soy flour, sugar substitute, salt, eggs, heavy cream, and club soda to make a smooth, thick, pancake-like batter. Spray pizza pans generously with the vegetable oil spray. Using a rubber spatula, spread the batter as thinly and evenly as possible over the 2 pans. Bake for about 12 to 15 minutes, or until lightly golden brown and firm to touch.

To make chicken:
In a large sauté pan or wok, heat oil over high heat. Season the chicken with salt, pepper, cayenne, cumin, and garlic, and add to the hot oil. Next add the peppers and onions, remove pan from the heat, and add

tequila. Cook for about 5 minutes or until chicken is cooked thoroughly. Keep warm.

To assemble:
Cut 1 flat bread into 4 pieces. On 2 pieces, layer cheese, cooked chicken mixture, and more cheese, and cover with the other 2 pieces. (Wrap the other flatbread and freeze for another use).

Lastly, melt butter until very hot in a sauté pan over medium-high heat. Add quesadillas and cook for about 2 minutes on each side until toasty and the cheese is melted. Cut quesadillas into 3 pieces each and serve. Garnish with cilantro and scallions, and serve with salsa picante, guacamole, and sour cream, if desired.

DIETER'S DELIGHT

½ cup Sauza tequila
4 fresh peach slices
4 fresh strawberries
8 lettuce leaves
1 large scoop cottage cheese

Marinate the fresh peach slices and strawberries in ½ cup tequila for several minutes. Arrange several leaves of lettuce in a large stemmed glass and place a large scoop of cottage cheese in the center. Alternate peach slices and strawberries around the cottage cheese. Serves 1.

STUFFED TOMATOES

1 tbsp. tequila
4 large ripe tomatoes
2 7-oz. cans tuna, drained
8 slices crisply cooked bacon
½ tsp. salt
½ tsp. pepper

2 hard-cooked eggs, chopped
½ cup mayonnaise
parsley for garnish

Wash and dry the tomatoes. Remove a slice 1 inch from the top of each tomato. Carefully scoop out the inside of each tomato, leaving a shell. In a small mixing bowl, combine the remaining ingredients except for the parsley, and mix thoroughly. Stuff each tomato with the tuna mixture and garnish with parsley. Serves 4.

MEXICAN BEAN DIP

2 tbsp. tequila
6 slices bacon, chopped into 1-inch pieces
1 29-oz. can refried pinto beans
1½ tsp. garlic powder
1 small onion, finely chopped
1 tsp. black pepper
2 serrano chilies, finely chopped

In a heavy saucepan, fry the bacon until nearly crisp. Add the beans, garlic, onion, pepper, chilies, and tequila. Stir thoroughly to combine and add salt sparingly to taste. Serve warm with tortilla chips. Yields four cups.

VEGETABLE DIP

2 tsp. tequila
1 cup mayonnaise
1 tsp. garlic powder
1 tbsp. lemon juice
¼ tsp. curry powder

Mix all ingredients and chill well. Serve with assorted raw vegetable sticks and slices.

SWEET POTATO SALAD

2 tbsp. tequila
2 tbsp. brown sugar
1 lb. sweet potatoes, boiled with skins, drained, peeled, and mashed
4 stalks celery, chopped
4 hard-boiled eggs, chopped
4 small green onions, chopped
salt
freshly ground pepper to taste
¼ to ½ cup mayonnaise to moisten

In a large bowl, dissolve the brown sugar in tequila. Add all the remaining ingredients, mix well, and serve warm. Serves 6.

TEQUILA SAUSAGE

½ cup tequila
¼ cup vegetable oil
1 lb. Italian sweet sausage

Heat the oil in a skillet, and add the sausage. Cook on each side for approximately 10 to 12 minutes. When browned, drain off the oil and add the tequila. Cover and let the sausage simmer for five to six minutes. Serve immediately. Serves 2.

VANILLA MOUSSE

1 tbsp. tequila
1 pint heavy cream
⅓ cup powdered sugar
1½ tsp. vanilla
2 stiffly beaten egg whites

Whip the cream until it will just hold its shape. Add the sugar and vanilla, and lightly fold in the tequila and beaten egg whites. Pour into a mold or individual serving dishes and freeze. Serves 4.

APPLESAUCE PIE

¼ cup tequila
16 graham crackers, crushed
4 lb. butter, softened
2 cups applesauce
whipped cream for serving

Mix the graham crackers and butter. Press into a pie tin to form a crust. Pour the chilled applesauce and tequila into the crust and bake 20 minutes at 375°F. Cool overnight in the refrigerator and top with whipped cream just before serving.

KEY LIME MARGARITA PIE

For crust:
½ cup pretzels, finely crushed
½ cup graham crackers, finely crushed
¼ cup sugar
⅓ cup butter, melted

For filling:
2 tbsp. tequila
1 14-oz. can sweetened condensed milk
⅓ cup frozen limeade concentrate, thawed
1 tbsp. orange liqueur
few drops green food coloring, optional
1 cup heavy cream
lime slices for garnish

Preheat oven to 375°F.

To make the pretzel crust:
Combine the crushed pretzels, graham crackers, sugar, and melted butter. Once the mixture is combined, spread evenly into a 9-inch pie tin. Press the mixture in the tin onto the bottom and the sides to form a firm, even crust. Bake for 5 minutes until the edges are lightly browned. Let shell cool until needed.

For the filling:
Using a large mixing bowl, combine the sweetened condensed milk, limeade, tequila, orange liqueur, and food coloring if desired, until all ingredients are well mixed. In a medium-size bowl, beat the heavy cream until soft peaks form. Fold the whipped cream into the lime and tequila mixture. Spoon the filling into the pie shell, cover, and freeze for 4 hours or until firm.

To serve:
Let pie stand for 10 minutes after coming out of freezer. Slice pie and garnish with lime slices.

MARGARITA POPSICLES

2 tbsp. tequila
¾ cup sugar
¾ cup fresh lime juice
½ cup water
2 tbsp. fresh lemon juice
2 tbsp. fresh orange juice
2 tbsp. orange liqueur (recommended: Grand Marnier)
kosher salt, for garnish

Special equipment: 4 small cups (such as Dixie cups), 4 popsicle sticks.
Combine sugar, lime juice, water, lemon juice, and orange juice in a small saucepan over medium heat. Cook, stirring, until sugar dissolves. Remove from heat and allow to cool. Once cool, transfer to a blender with tequila, orange liqueur, and lime wedge and process until smooth. Pour

into the cups and cover the top of each cup with foil. Place a popsicle stick in the center of each cup (down through foil, which will hold it in place). Freeze until hard, preferably overnight. Remove from freezer and run cup under warm water to loosen popsicle. Garnish with kosher salt and serve.

AVOCADO SOUP

¼ cup tequila, preferably aged
1 lb. Hass avocados (about 4), peeled and chopped
2 tbsp. roughly chopped fresh cilantro leaves
6 cups homemade chicken stock, or low-sodium canned chicken stock, chilled
1 serrano or jalapeño pepper, seeded and veined, minced
1 cup freshly squeezed orange juice (2 oranges)
coarse salt
½ tsp. grated orange zest
1 watermelon, for serving

To make soup:
In a blender, combine avocado, cilantro, ¾ cup chicken stock, and serrano pepper. Add orange juice, tequila, salt, zest, and remaining 5¼ cups chicken stock. Blend until smooth, in 2 batches if necessary. Strain through a sieve.

To serve:
Cut watermelon in half, crosswise. Hollow out one half of the watermelon, forming a tureen. Seed flesh, and cut into ½-inch cubes. Pour soup into watermelon, and garnish with watermelon cubes. Reserve remaining ½ watermelon for another use.

MARGARITA CHEESECAKE

3 tbsp. gold tequila
1¼ cups vanilla wafer cookie crumbs
¼ cup unsalted butter, melted
3 8-oz. packages cream cheese, at room temperature
2 cups sour cream
1¼ cup sugar
3 tbsp. Grand Marnier
3 tbsp. freshly squeezed lime juice
2 tsp. grated lime peel
4 large eggs
very thin lime slices, for garnish

Preheat oven to 350°F. Mix cookie crumbs and butter in medium bowl until blended. Press mixture onto bottom and 1 inch up sides of 9-inch diameter spring-form pan with 2¾-inch high sides. Refrigerate while preparing filling.

Using electric mixer, beat cream cheese in large bowl until fluffy. Add 1 cup sour cream, 1 cup sugar, Grand Marnier, tequila, lime juice, and lime peel; beat until well blended. Add eggs one at a time, beating just until blended after each addition.

Pour filling into crust. Bake until center is softly set, about 50 minutes. Maintain oven temperature. Mix remaining 1 cup sour cream, ¼ cup sugar, and 1 tbsp. lime juice in small bowl. Pour over cheesecake. Using spatula, smooth top. Bake cheesecake 5 minutes longer. Transfer pan to rack and cool completely. Refrigerate until well chilled, at least 4 hours or overnight. Run knife around pan sides to loosen cake. Remove pan sides. Garnish cake with lime slices.

MARGARITA CHICKEN

⅔ cup tequila
4 bone-in chicken breast halves
1 10-oz. can frozen margarita mix, thawed (recommended: Bacardi)

½ cup fresh cilantro leaves, chopped
2 tbsp. chicken seasoning (preferably McCormick's Grill Mates)

Rinse the chicken breasts and pat dry; set aside.
In a small bowl, combine the remaining ingredients. Place the chicken and marinade in large, resealable plastic bag. Squeeze out the air and seal. Let marinate in the refrigerator for 1 to 2 hours.
Set up the grill for direct cooking over medium heat and oil grate when ready to start cooking. Remove the chicken from the refrigerator and let sit at room temperature for 30 minutes.
Place chicken on hot, oiled grill and cook 5 to 6 minutes per side, or until done.
Indoors: Preheat oven to 350°F. Prepare chicken breasts as directed. Roast chicken breasts in preheated oven for 35 to 40 minutes.

TEQUILA STEAK FAJITA

⅛ cup tequila
juice of 3 lemons
½ tbsp. red chili pepper flakes
1 tsp. chili powder
4 cloves garlic, crushed
⅔ lb. flank steak
2 tsp. canola oil
1 red bell pepper, sliced
1 yellow bell pepper, sliced
½ red onion, sliced
½ tsp. salt
¼ tsp. pepper
4 6-inch corn tortillas, warmed
1 cup chopped fresh cilantro leaves

Mix the lemon juice, tequila, pepper flakes, chili powder, and garlic in a medium-sized plastic container. Place the steak in the container, cover, and marinate in the refrigerator for at least 45 minutes.

Heat canola oil in a large nonstick sauté pan over medium heat. Add bell peppers and onion and sauté until crisp tender. Remove from pan, set aside, and keep warm. Remove steak from marinade and discard marinade. Sauté steak in the sauté pan for about 5 minutes on each side or until cooked through. Remove steak from the pan and slice into thin strips. Return steak strips, bell peppers, and onion to pan and warm through for about 1 minute. Season with salt and pepper, to taste. Divide steak mixture evenly among the warmed tortillas. Garnish each with ¼ cup cilantro and serve.

TEQUILA SHRIMP WITH GARLIC AND GUAJILLO CHILE

1½ oz. olive oil
2 cloves elephant garlic, sliced
2 oz. sliced guajillo chile
24 jumbo shrimp, peeled and deveined
juice of 1 lemon
2 tomatoes, diced
2 oz. tequila
4 oz. butter
chive sprigs for garnish

In a large skillet, heat the olive oil, add the garlic, and sauté until golden brown. Add the sliced chile and continue mixing until the oil has taken on the color of the chile.

Add the shrimp to the hot pan and sauté for 3 minutes. Add the lemon juice and the tomatoes. Add the tequila to the shrimp and carefully flambé. Cook until the alcohol burns out. On low heat, add the butter and swirl until the sauce slightly thickens.

To serve, plate the shrimp in the center of each plate and add the sauce in the center. Garnish each plate with chive sprigs.

TEQUILA MARINATED LONDON BROIL

1 cup tequila
1 jalapeño pepper, seeded
1 clove garlic
1 cup teriyaki sauce
¼ cup sesame oil, optional
¼ cup Worcestershire sauce
¼ tsp. kosher salt
¼ tsp. freshly ground black pepper
3½ pounds London broil
cilantro leaves for garnish

In a blender, combine all ingredients except London broil. Process until smooth. Place London broil in a nonreactive container and pour marinade over top, turning it to coat. Refrigerate for at least 4 to 6 hours before cooking.

Preheat grill to high.

Place London broil on white-hot grill and cook for 4 to 5 minutes on each side, flipping the steak 4 times (cooking time will vary with thickness of the steak).

Let steak rest for at least 10 minutes before thinly slicing against the grain of the meat and on a bias for wide but thin slices. Garnish with fresh cilantro.

QUESO FLAMEADO

12 to 18 oz. panela cheese
½ cup flour
¼ cup olive oil
1 cup gold tequila
lime juice to taste

Slice the cheese ½ inch thick and place in a bowl of ice water for about 5 minutes. Pat the cheese dry and dust with the flour, shaking off any excess.

Heat a large, cast-iron skillet over high heat. Add the oil and fry the cheese, turning once, until golden brown. Use caution! Standing far enough back so you do not get near the flames, ignite the tequila. Let the flames die out.

Remove the cheese and tequila to a platter and finish with a sprinkling of lime juice. Serve with pickled chipotle peppers and warm corn tortillas.

MARGARITA MELON SALAD

2 shots tequila
juice of 2 limes
2 tbsp. orange liqueur
3 tsp. sugar
½ cantaloupe, seeded and cubed
¼ honeydew melon, seeded and cubed
¼ small watermelon, cubed

Combine lime juice, tequila, liqueur, and sugar in a bowl. Add melons and toss to coat with tequila and lime. Serve in shallow bowls.

Note: Many markets sell halved melons and wedges of watermelon, making it easy to prepare this salad closer to desired amounts.

SMOKE DADDY BEANS

¼ cup tequila
2 cups BBQ sauce, your favorite
3 cups ketchup
2 cups brown sugar
2 10-lb. cans ranch-style beans, undrained
6 cups diced onions

2 cups beef brisket scraps, ⅜- to ½-inch pieces
1½ cups pork shoulder, chopped ⅜- to ½-inch
1 tbsp. ground black pepper
¼ cup yellow mustard
¼ cup cilantro leaves, julienne
1 tsp. chipotle pepper puree
1 tsp. minced garlic
1 tsp. chili powder
1 tsp. ground cumin

Heat oven to 350°F.

Mix all the ingredients together in a cast-iron pan or any oven-safe pan. Bake for about 2 hours, then finish in the smoker for another 2 hours.

SPICY TEQUILA-SPIKED CHERRY TOMATOES

¼ cup plus 2 tbsp. unaged tequila
1 lb. small cherry tomatoes (about 35)
2 tsp. unflavored gelatin
⅔ cup vegetable-juice cocktail, such as V-8, or tomato juice
2 jalapeños, seeded and minced
2 tbsp. minced white onion
2 tbsp. minced cilantro
½ tsp. salt
½ tsp. celery salt
cilantro leaves, for garnish (optional)

Cut off ¼ inch from the blossom end (opposite of stem end) of each tomato, and with a ¼ tsp. measure carefully scoop out the seeds.

In a small saucepan, sprinkle the gelatin over the vegetable-juice cocktail or tomato juice and let stand 1 minute to soften. Heat the mixture over moderately low heat, stirring until gelatin is dissolved.

Remove the pan from the heat, and stir in the jalapeño and all remaining ingredients except tomatoes. Cool filling slightly.

Using a small spoon and holding each tomato over saucepan, spoon filling into tomatoes, arranging tomatoes on a platter as filled. Chill tomatoes, covered, 4 hours or until filling is set, and up to 1 day.

Garnish each tomato with a cilantro leaf (optional).

—*From* Gourmet

GRILLED POUND CAKE WITH PINEAPPLE SALSA AND TEQUILA WHIPPED CREAM

For tequila whipped cream:
1 tbsp. tequila (preferably reposado or anejo)
¾ cup heavy (whipping) cream
3 tbsp. confectioners' sugar
¼ tsp. ground cinnamon

For pineapple salsa:
2 cups fresh pineapple, cut into ½-inch cubes
3 tbsp. thinly slivered fresh mint or lemon verbena
1 to 2 jalapeño peppers, seeded and minced (for a hotter salsa, leave the seeds in)
2 tbsp. fresh lime juice, or more to taste
1 tbsp. light brown sugar, or more to taste

For cake:
8 slices pound cake (each ½ inch thick)
2 to 3 tbsp. unsalted butter, melted
4 fresh mint sprigs, for garnish

To make whipped cream:
Place the cream in a chilled mixer bowl or a large metal bowl. Beat with a mixer until soft peaks form, starting on slow speed and gradually increasing to high speed. The total beating time will be 6 to 8 minutes. When soft peaks have formed, add the confectioners' sugar, cinnamon,

and tequila. Continue beating the cream until stiff peaks form, about 2 minutes longer. Don't overbeat the cream or it will start to turn to butter. The tequila whipped cream can be made several hours ahead. Refrigerate it, covered, until ready to serve.

To make salsa:
Place the pineapple, mint, jalapeño, lime juice, and brown sugar in a nonreactive mixing bowl, but don't mix them until 5 minutes before ready to serve. Taste for seasoning, adding more lime juice and/or brown sugar as necessary.

Lightly brush each slice of pound cake with butter on both sides. Grill the pound cake, outdoors or on a grill pan, until lightly toasted. If desired, rotate each slice a quarter turn after 1 minute to create a handsome crosshatch of grill marks. You may need to cook the pound cake slices in more than one batch.

To assemble:
Place the pound cake slices on plates. Top each serving with a spoonful of pineapple salsa and a dollop of tequila whipped cream, garnish with a sprig of mint, and serve at once. Serves 4.

TEQUILA SHRIMP

¼ cup tequila
1 lb. large shrimp, peeled and deveined
1 tbsp. olive oil
2 large cloves garlic, chopped
¼ cup chopped fresh cilantro
salt and pepper to taste

Heat oil in a large skillet over high heat. Add shrimp. Sauté quickly until almost done, then add garlic. Sauté for another minute, then remove completely from heat and add tequila. Allow alcohol to burn off briefly and carefully return to heat (there's a good chance there will be flames; be careful). Add cilantro and salt and pepper, stir briefly, and serve.

TEX WASABI'S KOI FISH TACOS

Main ingredients:
1 tbsp. tequila
juice of 1 lime
1 tsp. ground cumin
1 tsp. salt
1 tsp. black pepper
12 oz. cod or firm white fish, cut in 1-inch pieces
16 8-inch corn tortillas
6-8 oz. canola oil
4 oz. tempura flour
8 oz. prepared tempura batter made with cold water
6 oz. panko bread crumbs
1 cup shredded white cabbage
½ cup shredded red cabbage
3 tbsp. chopped cilantro leaves
¼ cup very thinly sliced red onion

For pico de gallo:
4 roma tomatoes, diced
2 tbsp. chopped cilantro leaves
½ red onion, minced
1 tsp. minced garlic
1 jalapeño, seeded and minced
juice of 1 lime
salt and pepper

For tequila lime aioli:
3 tbsp. premium tequila
juice of 1 lime
8 oz. sour cream
¼ cup milk
2 tsp. minced garlic
½ tsp. ground cumin
2 tbsp. minced cilantro leaves

salt and pepper

To make pico de gallo:
In a bowl, mix all ingredients, season with salt and pepper, and refrigerate for 1 hour for flavors to meld.

To make tequila lime aioli:
In small bowl, combine all ingredients and chill for 1 hour. Season with salt and pepper to taste.

To make fish tacos:
In a medium bowl, combine lime juice, tequila, cumin, salt, and pepper; mix thoroughly. Add the fish and toss to coat. Marinate for 10 minutes. Warm tortillas on grill or pan. Cover with a towel to keep warm. In a medium Dutch oven, heat the canola oil to 350°F.

Remove fish from marinade, shake off excess, dredge in tempura flour, and dunk in cold tempura mixed batter. Roll in panko bread crumbs, pressing panko onto fish. One by one, add fish to oil, making sure to keep the fish pieces separated. Fry for 4–5 minutes, or until light golden brown. Remove and drain on paper towels.

Mix cabbage, cilantro, and onion. Stack 2 tortillas; place ⅛ of fish on top of each, and top with cabbage mixture, pico de gallo, and tequila lime aioli. Serve immediately.

TEQUILA CURED SALMON

3 cups tequila
4 cups brown sugar
6 cups salt
2 red onions, peeled and roughly chopped
2 carrots, peeled and roughly chopped
3 red peppers, cored, seeded, and roughly chopped
3 green peppers, cored, seeded, and roughly chopped
3 yellow peppers, cored, seeded, and roughly chopped
2 lemons, cut into 8 wedges

2 limes, cut into 8 wedges
1 8-10 lb. salmon fillet
1 cup black pepper, freshly ground
Sweet corn cakes (cachapas) or Cuban crackers, suggested for serving

Mix together sugar and salt. Puree onions, carrots, peppers, lemons, and limes together in a food processor. Combine sugar mixture and puree. Add tequila. Pour half of the mixture into the bottom of a large pan. Coat flesh side of salmon with pepper. Place salmon in the pan (skin side up). Cover salmon with remaining mixture and place another pan on top with plenty of weight. Refrigerate for 2 days.

To serve, slice thinly and place on top of sweet corn cakes, cachapas, or Cuban crackers.

70
TEQUILA PRODUCERS

In order to control the production and labeling of tequila, the Norma Oficial Mexicana (NOM) was created in 1978. NOM monitors the production of tequila and is similar to the French "Appalachian Controller." In order to display the tequila label, the agave must be grown and processed in the state of Jalisco or in the narrow region from the surrounding states of Guanajuato, Tamaulipas, Michoacan, and Nayarit.

4 Copas
1800
Agabe Tequilana
Asom Broso
Bacanora de Sonora
Buen Amigo Brands
Buscadores
Cabo Wabo
Casa Herradura
Casa Noble
Chinaco
Cielo Hand Crafted
Corporacion Ansan
Corzo
Del Maguey Mezcals

Destiladora Azteca de Jalisco
Destiladora Rubio
Destileria La Fortuna
Destillados Ole
Don Amado Mezcal
Don Cuco Sotol
Don Eduardo
Don Fernando
Dos Lunas
El Duende
El Reformador
El Señorio Mezcal
El Tesoro
Fina Estampa
Hacienda la Capilla
Hacienda los Magueyes
Heaven Hill Distilleries
Jose Cuervo
La Certeza
La Cofradia Distillery
Margaritaville
Metl 2012 Mezcal
Oro Azul
Oro de Jalisco
Partida tequila
Penca Azul
Pepe Lopez
Reserva del Señor Almendrado
Scorpion Mezcal and Mezcals de Oaxaca
Sierra
Skyrocket Distillers
Sotol Hacienda de Chihuahua
Sotol Sereque
Tequila 0.720
Tequila 1921
Tequila 3030

Tequila 33
Tequila 7 Leguas
Tequila Agave Dos Mil
Tequila Amate
Tequila Caballo Moro
Tequila Campanario
Tequila Canicas
Tequila Cascahuin
Tequila Cazadores
Tequila Chaya
Tequila Corazon de Agave
Tequila Corralejo
Tequila Don Nacho
Tequila Don Roberto
Tequila Don Tacho
Tequila Don Valente
Tequila D'Reyes
Tequila El Charro
Tequila El Tequileno

130

TEQUILA WEBSITES
AND RESOURCES

http://1800tequila.com
http://www.4copas.com/

http://www.acumbaro.com/
http://www.agabetequilana.com
http://www.agavedosmil.com/
http://agavero.com/
http://www.ahatoro.com/
http://www.allieddomecq.com
http://www.almendrado.com/
http://www.amate.com/
http://www.amatitense.com
http://www.asombrosotequila.com/
http://www.awzwoltinternational.com/tequila.html

http://www.bartonbrands.com/montezuma2.html
http://www.beyondtequila.com
http://buenamigo.com/
http://www.buscadorestequila.com/

http://www.cabowabo.com/
http://www.californiatequila.com/

http://www.canicas.com
http://www.casagoytia.com/
http://www.casanoble.com/
http://www.cascoviejo.com.mx/
http://www.cazadores.com/
http://www.cesarmonterrey.com/
http://www.chayatequila.com/
http://www.Chinacotequila.com
http://www.corzo.com/

http://www.destiladorarubio.com/
http://www.destileria501.com/
http://www.DonAmado.com/
http://www.DonEduardo.com/
http://www.DonTacho.com/
http://www.DosLunas.com/tequila/

http://www.elagaveartesanal.com/
http://www.elcapricho.com.au/
http://elcharrotequila.com/
http://www.elduendetequila.com/http://www.elmayor.com/
http://www.elreformador.com/
http://www.elsenorio.com/
http://www.ElTesorotequila.com/lpa/?lparefer=/

http://www.FinaEstampatequila.com/

http://www.Haciendalacapilla.com/
http://www.heaven-hill.com/brands-tequila.html
http://www.Herenciamexicana.com.mx/Products.htm
http://www.herradura.com/

http://www.insignia.com.mx/
http://www.itequila.org/

http://www.jarroviejo.com.mx/

http://www.jbwagoners.com/
http://www.jimador.com.mx/
http://josecuervoplatino.com/
http://juareztequila.com/

http://www.lacerteza.com/
http://www.lapazproducts.com/
http://www.ley925.com/
http://www.losabuelos.com/
http://www.losdanzantes.com/

http://www.m3w3.com.mx/tequilaRevolucion/
http://www.margaritavilletequila.com/
http://www.mezcal.com/
http://www.Milagrotequila.com/

http://www.nuevoedge.com

http://Oroazultequila.com/
http://www.Orodejalisco.com/

http://www.patronspirits.com/
http://www.partidatequila.com/
http://www.pencazul.com/
http://www.pepelopez.com/
http://www.pirichona.com/
http://www.Pocotequila.com/antour/aguila.html

http://www.Realhacienda.com/

http://www.sallys-place.com/beverages/spirits/tequila.htm
http://www.saltlemon.com/
http://www.sanmatias.com/Productos/pv.aspx
http://www.sanmatias.com/Productos/rs.aspx
http://www.Sauzatequila.com/login.asp
http://www.Sierra-tequila.de/

http://www.Solazultequila.com/

---

http://www.TarantulaAzul.com/
http://www.tequila.net/
http://www.tequila0720.com/
http://www.tequila1921.com/
http://www.tequila3030.com/old_version/
http://www.tequila33.com/
http://tequilaArette.com/
http://www.tequileradearandas.com/
http://www.tequilaCampanario.com/
http://www.tequilaCampoazul.com/
http://www.tequilaCasaReal.com/
http://www.tequilaCentinela.com.mx/
http://www.tequilaChamucos.com/
http://www.tequilaCofradia.com/
http://www.tequilaCorazon.com/_splash.cfm?ref=/index.cfm
http://www.tequilaCorralejo.com/
http://www.tequilasDeladona.com/
http://www.tequilasDelsenor.com.mx/
http://www.tequilaDonNacho.com/
http://www.tequilaDonRoberto.com/
http://www.tequilaDonValente.com/
http://www.tequilaEsperanto.com/
http://www.tequilaEspolon.com/
http://www.tequilaHaciendadeoro.com/entrada/entrada.php
http://tequilajones.com/html/find_tequila.html
http://www.tequilalosgenerales.com/
http://www.tequilaMiravalle.com.mx/
http://www.tequilaMitierra.com.mx/
http://www.tequilaNacional.com/
http://www.tequilaOlmeca.com/
http://www.tequila-Orendain.com/
http://tequilaPurasangre.com/index800.htm
http://www.tequilaQuiote.com/
http://www.tequilarte.com/

http://www.tequila-Santafe.com.mx/
http://www.tequilaSieteleguas.com.mx/
http://www.tequilasource.com/
http://www.tequilaTresmujeres.com.mx/
http://www.tequilaxq.com.mx/
http://www.tequilazafarrancho.com/
http://www.tequileradearandas.com/
http://www.tequileraeltriangulo.com/
http://thebar.com/?primarysection=3&brand=8
http://www.Trago-tequila.com/
http://Tresriostequila.com/
http://www.tukys.com/
http://www.tikitequila.com/

http://www.vidatequila.com/
http://www.vincevineyards.com/

http://www.xxxtequila.com/

GLOSSARY

TOOLS YOU WILL NEED

Bar spoon: A long spoon for stirring cocktails or pitchers.

Blender: Blending drinks or crushing ice. Remember to save your blade by always pouring in the liquid before the ice.

Cocktail shaker and mixing/measuring glass: There are countless designs to choose from, but the standard is the Boston. It's a mixing glass that fits snugly into a stainless steel cone.

Ice bag: To crush ice, use a rubber mallet and a lint-free or canvas ice bag, often referred to as a Lewis Ice Bag.

Ice bucket: Should have a vacuum seal and the ability to hold three trays of ice.

Ice scoop/tongs/ice pick: Never use your hands to pick up ice; use a scoop or tongs. The ice pick can help you unstick ice or break it up.

Jigger/measuring glass: Glass or metal; all drinks should be made using these bar tools. Remember that drinks on the rocks and mixed drinks should contain no more than 2 oz. of alcohol.

Knife and cutting board: A sturdy board and a small, very sharp paring knife are essential to cutting fruit garnishes.

Muddler: Use this small wooden bat or pestle to crush fruit, herbs, or cracked ice. Muddlers come in all different sizes and are used for making Stixx drinks.

Napkins/coasters: To place a drink on, hold a drink with, and for basic convenience.

Pitcher of water: Keep it clean. Someone always wants water and you certainly will use it.

Pourer: A helpful way to pour directly into the glass. A lidded spout helps keep everything but the drink out.

Stirrers/straws: Use them to sip, stir, and mix drinks. Glass is preferred for the mixer/stirrer. They can be custom molded and come in all different shapes and colors. (www.brandedstirs.com/printabledrink-stirs.html)

Strainer: The strainer, quite simply, prevents ice from pouring out of the shaker. The two most common types in use are the Hawthorne and the Julep. The Hawthorne, with its distinctive coil rim, is most often used when pouring from the metal part of the Boston Shaker. The Julep is a perforated metal spoon-like strainer used when pouring from the glass part of the Boston.

Swizzle stick: A fancy stirrer, often with an establishment's name on it.

Wine/bottle opener: They come in all shapes and sizes; the best is the industry standard Waiter's opener. It opens cans as well as snaps off those bottle tops, and it has a sharp blade.

GLASSWARE

Brandy snifters: Smaller sizes of the glasses, which come in sizes ranging from 5½ to 22 oz., are perfect for serving cognac, liqueurs, and premium whiskeys. The larger sizes provide enough space for a noseful of aroma, and the small stems on large bowls allow a cupped hand to warm the liquid.

Champagne glass: A narrow version of the standard wine glass has a tapered bowl to prevent those tiny bubbles from escaping and is usually never more than half filled. Also preferable for any sparkling liquid, including ciders.

Cocktail or martini glass: Perfect for martinis and manhattans, remember that the stem is not just for show; it keeps hands from warming the drink. Available in 3 to 6 oz. sizes.

Coolers: These large-capacity tumblers are taller and hold a lot of ice for larger concoctions. They have become popular of late for nonalcoholic and extra-volume highballs.

Highball glass: Extremely versatile glass available in many sizes and used for almost any drink. Usually clear and tall, the most popular sizes range from 8 to 12 oz.

Hurricane glass: Tropical fruit drinks and Bloody Marys are perfectly suited for these 16 to 23 oz. tall, curved glasses.

Rocks glasses: These "old-fashioned" glasses hold from 6 to 10 oz. and are used for on-the-rocks presentations. Double rocks will run between 12 and 15 oz.

Shot glass: The old standby can also be used as a measuring glass and is a must for every bar.

MIXING TERMS

Build: In a glass full of ice, first pour in the liquor or spirit, then add the mixer. Add stirring/swizzle stick to stir the cocktail.

Fill: After you add ice and liquor or spirits, fill with mixer to within ¼ inch of the top.

Floating: To layer one ingredient on the top of a shot or cocktail.

Layering: Topping one ingredient over another.

TYPES OF DRINKS

Aperitif: A light alcohol drink served before lunch or dinner, sometimes bitter.

Blended drinks: Blended drinks consisting of ice, ice cream, and a variety of other ingredients blended until smooth though thick consistency.

Cobbler: A tall drink usually filled with crushed ice and garnished with fruit or mint.

Cream: Any drink made with ice cream, heavy cream, half-and-half, or any of the famous bottled cream drinks.

Crusta: Served in a wine glass with sugar-coated rim and the inside of the glass lined with a citrus rind.

Cups: A traditionally British category of wine-based drinks.

Daisy: An oversized cocktail sweetened with fruit syrup served over crushed ice.

Eggnog: A blend of milk or cream, beaten eggs, sugar, and liquor, usually rum, brandy, or whiskey; sometimes sherry topped with nutmeg.

Flip: Cold, creamy drinks made with eggs, sugar, alcohol, and citrus juice.

Highball: A tall drink usually served with whiskey and ginger ale. The favorite drink of many grandparents.

Grog: A rum-based drink made with fruit and sugar.

Julep: A tall, sweet drink usually made with bourbon, water, sugar, crushed ice, and occasionally mint. The most popular Julep being, of course, the Kentucky Derby's famous Mint Julep.

Mist: Any type of alcoholic beverage served over crushed ice.

Mojita: A Cuban-born drink prepared with sugar, muddled mint leaves, fresh lime juice, rum, ice, and soda water, and garnished with mint leaves.

Pousse-café: A drink made with layers created by floating liqueur according to their density.

Puff: Made with equal parts alcohol and milk topped with club soda.

Rickey: A cocktail made of alcohol (usually whiskey, lime juice, and soda water).

Shooter: A straight shot of alcohol, also sometimes called serving a drink "neat."

Sling: A tall drink made with lemon juice and sugar, topped with club soda.

Sours: Drinks made with lemon juice, sugar, and alcohol.

Stixx: Tall, muddled cocktails using different sized muddlers from six inches to twelve inches. Muddled cocktails are now made with herbs, fruits, spices, and a variety of ethnic and regional ingredients including beans, roots, and spices.

Toddy: Served hot, it's a mixture of alcohol, spices, and hot water.

Toppers: Blended drinks with ice cream or crushed ice; the thicker the better, which is why these drinks are served with a spoon and a straw. They are made using cordials, flavored rums, flavored vodkas, blended fresh fruits, and tropical juices. They are topped with crushed candy, fruits, nuts, and just about anything you can eat with a spoon.

HOW TO RIM YOUR GLASS

Coating the rim of a glass with salt, sugar, or any other like substance adds a decorative touch that improves the presentation of the cocktail. Simple steps:

- Moisten the rim of the glass (a lime wedge to rim a margarita; sugar for Kahlua or chocolate martini).
- Dip the rim in your ingredient of choice.
- Slowly turn the glass to ensure you coat evenly.
- Shake off any excess.
- Fill the glass with your prepared cocktail.

For more information and different cocktail rimmers, go to www. stirrings.com.

INDEX

B

Bad attitude, 15
Baha fog, 16
Baileys tequila cream, 16
Baja Tabasco shrimp, 247–248
Barking spider, 16
Bay City bomber, 17
BB gun, 17
Beach, 17
Beauty and the beast, 18
Bee sting, 18
Beergarita, 18
Benelyn, 19
Berry Medley, 19
Berta's special, 20
Bertha, 20
Besitos, 20
Big John's strawberry mango
   margarita, 21
Big red hooter, 21
Big spender, 21
Billionaire's margarita, 22
Bittersweet Steve on the rocks, 22
Black cat, 22
Black Mexican (hot), 22
Blackberry tequila, 23
Blanco martini, 23
Bleeding weasel, 23
Blitz, 24
Bloody bull, 24
Bloody hurricane, 24
Bloody Maria, 25
Bloody matador, 25
Bloody Pepe, 25
Blue agave mist, 26

Blue seven, 26
Blue sex, 26
Blue shark, 26
Blue smoke, 27
Bomshel, 27
Bon voyage, 27
Bonbon, 27
Bootlegger, 28
Border crossing, 28
Bowl hugger, 28
Brave bull, 29
Broken nose, 29
Brothel, 29
Bruja Mexicana, 30
Buen Amigo tequila, 10, 15, 17, 34,
   38, 43, 50, 54, 56, 63, 65, 81, 87,
   89, 92, 103, 109, 120, 121, 125,
   128, 129, 131, 132, 135, 137,
   140, 143, 144, 146, 158, 160,
   169, 170, 172, 178, 183, 184,
   192, 205, 210, 217, 218
Bumblebee keela, 30
Bunny bonanza, 30
Buttafuoco, 31

C

Cabo, 31
Cabo Wabo reposado tequila, 220
Cabo Wabo tequila, 220
Cactus banger, 31
Cactus berry, 32
Cactus bite, 32
Cactus kicker, 32
Café del Prado, 33
Caipicuervo, 33

D

T

Y

Z

ABOUT THE AUTHOR

Ray Foley, a former Marine with over thirty years of bartending and restaurant experience, is Founder and Publisher of *Bartender Magazine*. *Bartender Magazine* is the only magazine in the world specifically geared toward bartenders and is one of the very few primarily designed for servers of alcohol. *Bartender Magazine* is enjoying its twenty-ninth year. It currently has a circulation of over 148,000 and is steadily growing.

After serving in the United States Marine Corps and attending Seton Hall University, Ray entered the restaurant business as a bartender, which eventually led to his position as Assistant General Manager of The Manor in West Orange, New Jersey, where he managed over 350 employees.

In 1983, Ray left The Manor to devote his full efforts to *Bartender Magazine*. The circulation and exposure has grown from 7,000 to over 148,000 to date and has become the largest on-premise liquor magazine in the country.

Ray has been published in numerous articles throughout the country and has appeared on TV and radio shows.

He is also the founder of the Bartender Hall of Fame™, which honors the best bartenders throughout the United States not only for their abilities as mixologists, but for involvement in their communities as well.

In addition, Ray is the founder of The Bartenders' Foundation™ Incorporated. This nonprofit foundation has been set up to raise scholarship money for bartenders and their families. Scholarships awarded to bartenders can either be used to further their education or the education of their children.

Mr. Foley serves as a consultant to some of our nation's foremost distillers and importers. He is also responsible for naming and inventing new drinks for the liquor industry, including the Fuzzy Navel and the Royal Stretch.

Ray has one of the largest collections of cocktail recipe books in the world, dating back to the 1800s. He is one of the foremost collectors of cocktail shakers, with 368 shakers in his collection.

Ray is the author of Bartender Magazine's *Ultimate Bartender's Guide, Beer is the Answer . . . I Don't Remember the Question, The Ultimate Little Cocktail Book, The Ultimate Little Shooter Book, The Ultimate Little Martini Book, The Ultimate Little Blender Book, The Best Irish Drinks, X-Rated Drinks,* The *Vodka 1000, Bartending for Dummies,* and *How to Run a Bar for Dummies.*

Ray resides in New Jersey with his wife and partner of twenty-five years, Jackie, and their son, Ryan. He is also the father of three other wonderful and bright children: Raymond Pindar, William, and Amy.

Ray is foremost, and always will be, a bartender.

For more information, please contact Jackie Foley at *Bartender Magazine*, PO Box 158, Liberty Corner, NJ 07938. Telephone: (908) 766-6006; FAX: (908) 766-6607; email: barmag@aol.com; website: www.bartender.com.